How to Color-Tune Your Home

by
LOUIS CHESKIN
DIRECTOR, COLOR RESEARCH INSTITUTE OF AMERICA

REVISED EDITION

NK
2115
.C48
1962

QUADRANGLE BOOKS / CHICAGO
1962

HOW TO COLOR-TUNE YOUR HOME

To Vivian

Contents

CHAPTER ONE

THE COLORS IN YOUR HOME HAVE POWER

1. Why This Book   1

This book is meant to inform the reader about the extraordinary importance of color as a factor in human happiness and is especially designed to provide guidance for making your home a color-tuned, harmonious place for pleasurable living.

2. Color Study Is New   4

It is usually confined to highly technical literature. Here is your chance to get practical information in understandable language and to join in an intriguing adventure.

3. Color Is Not a Frill   6

The colors of the furnishings in your rooms are not frills, but vital psychological factors in your home and important elements in your emotional life.

4. An Experiment With Four Colors   9

In the red room normal activity was impossible because of over-stimulation. In the blue room the occupants were sluggish, and activity was below normal. The brilliant yellow room caused extreme eyestrain. There was no evidence of any abnormal reactions in the green room, although there were complaints of monotony.

5. We Eat With Our Eyes   11

The luncheons (under manipulated colored lights) were a failure, although the experiments were successful. They demonstrated that color has a real power over the digestive system.

6. Color With a Purpose   12

After the black boxes that were loaded into cars were painted a light green, complaints and absenteeism were reduced in a factory. The same principle applies to housework. Perhaps some magenta red in your home can make a major contribution to contentment.

7. Emotional Problems and Color   13

The blue-and-black environment undoubtedly aggravated the woman's psychic illness, while the red surroundings helped her toward normal behavior and happiness.

8. Visual Stimulants and Sedatives   19

All red hues are stimulating to some degree. The warmer the red—the more yellow it contains—the more aggressive and advancing it is. Blue is the coldest of colors. It is a psychological sedative for people who are inclined to be easily overstimulated and often depressing for the morose type of individual.

9. Bright or Muted Colors in Your Home?   23

Vibrant colors in great doses, without spaces that provide eye-relief, can be nerve-wracking. Normally, people feel most comfortable with combinations of diluted and bright colors, for example, magenta red used with a delicate or grayed green or burnt orange with tan and turquoise blue.

10. Every Color Has a Mate   24

Complementary colors are natural pairs in vision. If the complementary color is not present, the eye has a tendency to see it anyway. Complementary hues are physical and optical mates.

11. Your Basic Color   26

First find the color that is to dominate the room. Then, out of this color and its complementary, you can have dozens of shades, tints and tones, all of which comprise a normal family of colors that can be combined and tuned to stimulate or to relax and to provide pleasant home surroundings.

12. Balancing Your Color Diet 29

Just as your food must be varied and seasoned, so should colors. The basic major color that fits your personality must have some salt and pepper.

13. Color, Illumination and Temperature 31

You should be aware that colors reflect and absorb heat and light in accordance with their proximity (in terms of physics) to black or white. The darker the color the more heat and light it absorbs; the lighter, the more heat and light it reflects into the room. But always bear in mind that the psychological power of color is more important to you than its absorption or reflection of heat and light.

14. The Over-All Picture in Choosing Colors 33

You should be careful to choose specific colors that meet your psychological needs or those of the member of the family who is to be the occupant of the room; at the same time you should take into consideration the lighting and proportional and dimensional aspects of the interior.

15. Gray for Balance and Harmony 35

Gray plus magenta red appears to the eye very much like gray plus violet-blue. You can therefore use a violet gray or magenta gray in combination with magenta red, green and a soft-toned yellow, such as that of light or natural wood.

16. Composing Your Living Space 37

The right colors are not all you need in order to get the most out of a room. The arrangement of the furniture is important, and the style or character of the furniture pieces is a vital factor in planning your living space.

17. In the Hands of the "Experts" 39

Imagine that you are moving into a new home or apartment and have not yet read this book. You are guided by "experts" in decorating. But when the rooms are finished, you alternate between satisfaction and disappointment. Something's wrong somewhere. What could it be?

18. Analysis of the Newly Furnished Home 43

The bedroom in this new, unhappy home does not provide the inspiration for pleasure that a bedroom can and should provide.

18. Analysis of the Newly Furnished Home (Cont.)

The bathroom is too cold. The black-green living room walls
are impossible. The shouting wallpaper in the dining area is
driving the occupants out of the house. As far as contented living is concerned, this new home is a total loss.

19. Your New Home After Color-Tuning   47

A modern bathroom with the right colors can inspire a desire
to make oneself more attractive. A living room, with varied
harmonious and unified effects of form and color, can make its
contribution to relaxation. In the dining area, the proper colors
will be conducive to the enjoyment of food. All parts of this
home are correlated and coordinated, geared to creating an environment for happy living.

CHAPTER TWO

A COLOR PLAN FOR EACH TYPE OF ROOM

1. Your Living Room   51

Remember always that you can have in your living room all the
related colors you want or any of the colors that are available, as
long as they are based on complementaries. Consult the charts
to get the right combinations.

2. The Master Bedroom   55

The bedroom is the place for privacy and intimacy. In planning
the colors and the furnishings in your living room you have to
consider every member of your family and also your friends.
In planning your bedroom, you need to consider only yourself
and your husband. Portraits are not appropriate for a bedroom
because they violate its privacy. The ideal form of art for a bedroom is the nude. Never underestimate the importance of a bedroom.

3. The Dining Area   61

Dining rooms are fast disappearing, but dining will always be
with us, whether we eat in a space that is part of the living
room or part of the kitchen. Color has a tremendous effect in
two ways on your pleasure in dining: as part of the food and
as an element of the surroundings in which you eat.

4. Your Kitchen 66

The modern kitchen has nothing in common with grand-mother's, except that it, too, is used for preparing food. By introducing appropriate color, you can make a great contribution to the psychological benefits to be derived from your kitchen. The walls and floor are important in the kitchen, and that is where you are free to provide suitable effects without interfering with the functions of the food-preparing appliances.

5. The Nursery 70

Baby enjoys colors in their pure states—pure vibrant red and brilliant blue. Red is normally the favorite with infants as well as with older children. Your baby does not appreciate "baby pink" and "baby blue." These are for grown-ups.

6. The Study 72

A study that has simply designed furniture, proportionately arranged, with color of the right hue and tone on the walls, creates an atmosphere conducive to concentration and clear thinking.

7. The Playroom 76

Failure to apply scientific color principles in the playroom may be the seed from which can grow estrangement between parents and children. Even delinquency is a possible result.

8. The Home Workshop 78

Lighting comes not only directly from the light—daylight, incandescent bulb or fluorescent tube—but is also reflected from the surfaces in the interior: ceiling, walls, worktables, machines and other objects.

9. The Guest Room 81

The guest room should be looked upon as a combination living room and bedroom. You shouldn't be subjective in choosing the colors for this room. Your own favorite color combination may not be pleasing to most of your visitors.

10. What Colors Should a Brunette Have in Her Room? 88

If you are a brunette and are striving to emphasize that fact, the background in your room should be light in tone or rich and vibrant.

11. What Colors Should You Have If You Are Brown-Haired?

89

If you have brown hair and are of medium complexion, you are free to go on an emotional binge as far as color is concerned. You should make your color choice on the basis of getting emotional satisfaction and meeting the physical conditions of your room.

12. What Colors Should a Redhead Have in Her Room?

91

If you are a redhead, green is your background color. A cool blue-green is ideal for your walls. Your hair will vibrate against it. The blue-green will make you look most attractive.

13. What Colors Should a Blonde Have in Her Room?

92

If your goal is to play up your blonde hair, a blue background will do it for you.

14. What Colors Should the Mature White-Haired Person Have in Her Room?

93

Surround yourself with vibrant colors to dramatize your white hair, to make yourself feel young in spirit. Watch the favorable effect a brilliant background will have on other peoples' attitudes toward you.

CHAPTER THREE

PSYCHOLOGICAL AND SOCIAL FACTORS IN COLOR AND DESIGN PREFERENCES

1. Conditioned Color Reactions

95

We know that the love for red is spontaneous. A negative reaction to black is equally natural. However, a person can be conditioned to react against red or, on the other hand, to react pleasurably to black.

2. Ego-Involvement, Prestige Identification and Your Libido

100

The young lady exhibited conflict between three powerful motives. The fuchsia flattered her complexion and was therefore related to ego-involvement. The chartreuse was in fashion and

2. Ego-Involvement, Prestige Identification and Your Libido (Cont.)

so aided prestige indentification. The turquoise dress, she felt, was beautiful. This emotion involved libidinous expression.

3. Phobias and Fetishes—Do You Have Any? 104

A strong fear of or aversion to a color is classified as a phobia. Green phobias are much more rare than phobias to red, yellow or blue. There are individuals who have an abnormally strong attraction to a specific color. "Blue was a fetish with her. The fetishism was brought out even more glaringly when I was at her apartment for dinner."

4. The Psychology of Black, White and Gray 107

Black makes adjacent colors appear more vibrant and beautiful. White, too, enhances other colors. Gray is neutral—to say that one likes gray is actually to express no preference. Don't try to judge personality by the colors people say they prefer.

5. Wallpaper: Its Psychological Aspect 108

Wallpapers with patterns of imaginary scenes and fairy-tale motifs, or of animals, fish, birds or butterflies, are excellent for baby's room if they are hung as murals. For adults, these razzle-dazzle wallpapers are eyesores and psychological irritants and may do more harm than would be thought possible.

6. Functional Design and Your Emotions 110

In functional design beauty and utility are one. Modern furniture design is simple and passive in character. It is smooth and soft producing an atmosphere of restfulness. It meets the psychological needs of our times.

7. Should You Get Modern Furniture? 113

"Why did I think I wanted traditional furniture?" you will ask yourself after you have thought about furniture rationally. The chief reason probably goes back to your early childhood. Traditional furniture has a number of psychological appeals.

8. Pictures, Sculpture and Ceramics for the Home 115

Pictures, sculpture and ceramics, because they are not bound by physical functions, are diverse in shape and proportion. A variety arouses interest and provides stimulation as well as appropriate colors. You may wish to paint your own pictures and do your own modeling.

9. Color in the Home of the Future   121

The home of the future, if it is to meet the psychological and
social needs of people living in an atomic age, will contain little
that is traditional and characteristic of a bygone age. We must
take a forward step in the art of living.

CHAPTER FOUR

THE FOUR SIDES OF COLOR: PHYSICAL, CHEMICAL, PHYSIOLOGICAL AND PSYCHOLOGICAL

1. Physical Aspects of Color   125

The belief in one or the other of two half-truths—one that color
is light, the other that color is pigment—is responsible for many
of the difficulties and perplexities that beset workers in color.
Color resides in both light and substance at the same time. Color
is a manifestation of the relationship between light and matter.

2. Chemical Aspects of Color   131

For mixing, colors must have chemical affinity. Always remember that although pigment color depends on light, it is chemical
in nature, and that a color, like love, may be either permanent
or fugitive.

3. Physiological Aspects of Color   133

The human eye is anatomically and physiologically equipped
to receive all waves of the visible spectrum in their totality
(white light) as well as the individual components of this part
of the spectrum (colors).

4. Psychological Aspects of Color   135

Perhaps the best way to understand the nature of color is to
recognize that every hue has a mate and a family. The complementary hue is the mate, and the related values—shades, tints
and tones—are the family. Color preference tests indicate that
colors normally affect people in accordance with specific laws.

CHAPTER FIVE

TOOLS FOR COLOR PLANNING

1. How to Use the Color Charts   143

Charts 1 and 7 are placed opposite each other for a reason: they
are a complementary set of colors. Any color or colors on chart

1. How to Use the Color Charts (Cont.)

1 combined in a color scheme with any other color or colors on either chart 1 or chart 7 will make an agreeable color scheme.

2. Mixing the Colors in Paint   147

The 9 secondary hues and the 288 tints, tones and shades can be mixed from the three primary hues, black and white.

ILLUSTRATIONS   *following page 150*

INTERIOR I. *The Author's Living Room.* Color plan is based on Complementary Color Charts No. 4 and No. 10.

INTERIOR II. *The Author's Kitchen.* Color plan is based on Complementary Color Charts No. 4 and No. 10.

INTERIOR III. *The Author's Recreation Room.* Color plan is based on Complementary Color Charts No. 3 and No. 9.

INTERIOR IV. *Living Room.* Color plan is based on Complementary Color Charts No. 2 and No. 8.

INTERIOR V. *Living Room.* Color plan is based on Complementary Color Charts No. 2 and No. 8.

INTERIOR VI. *Family Room.* Color plan is based on Complementary Color Charts No. 6 and No. 12.

INTERIOR VII. *Dinette.* Color plan is based on Complementary Color Charts No. 3 and No. 9.

INTERIOR VIII. *Living Room.* Color plan is based on Complementary Color Charts No. 1 and No. 7.

INTERIOR IX. *Kitchen.* Color plan is based on Complementary Color Charts No. 3 and No. 9.

INTERIOR X. *Kitchen.* Color plan is based on Complementary Color Charts No. 3 and No. 9.

INTERIOR XI. *Bedroom.* Color plan is based on Complementary Color Charts No. 5 and No. 11.

INTERIOR XII. *Living Room.* Color plan is based on Complementary Color Charts No. 4 and No. 10.

COLOR CHARTS

Complementary Charts No. 1 and No. 7.
Complementary Charts No. 2 and No. 8.
Complementary Charts No. 3 and No. 9.
Complementary Charts No. 4 and No. 10.
Complementary Charts No. 5 and No. 11.
Complementary Charts No. 6 and No. 12.

INDEX   199

INTRODUCTION

Of Ideas and Things

After reading this book you will have many ideas about color for your home, each of which will help you select proper and correct colors.

You may decide that you want different color schemes for each room of your home based on your family's choices. By consulting the color charts in this book you will know that the colors you choose are optically balanced, pleasing to the eye and psychologically satisfying.

You will learn to choose one color as dominant in a room and a complementary color as accent. You will also learn how to decide on a delicate tint, a light tone or a deep tone—and where to use and where not to use vibrant, pure hues.

Where paint is required, the color charts will provide guidance. This book gives information on the primary colors and on how to mix any or all of the three hundred colors shown in the color charts. Where large areas are involved, you will probably want to reduce the color intensity even beyond that shown in the charts.

You will have a clear idea of how to use color effectively after reading this book, but ideas are not the same as things. You may not always be able to get the things for your home —such as draperies, furniture, etc.—in the right colors. The scientific application of color is still not widespread and most producers of consumer products have little knowledge about color. But you *can* get the quality, serviceability and color you seek in some products.

At the Color Research Institute we are continually doing research on various products for the home. Not only are we concerned with colors, but with the quality and service-ability of the products, too. We do this work for manufacturers who are enlightened enough to try to provide you with the kind of items you want most—and to make them as attractive and durable as you desire. In this way we hope to translate our research into your satisfaction. And we have achieved a notable success in this field.

We come into contact with many different kinds of products of a competing nature. Many of these are designed for use in the home. Some are outstanding and I want you to know about them. In particular, information about three types of home furnishings may interest you: laminated plastic surfacing material, furniture and folding doors.

For example, in your kitchen you need a long life, heavy duty counter. On your dinette table you may want a top that can take heavy, daily use without being damaged. You may want your coffee table to be mar-proof. At the same time, you want the right color. Laminated plastic surfacing material is ideal for these uses.

A high-grade laminated plastic is a high pressure, decorative, laminated plastic. It is hard and smooth, highly resistant to wear and scratching, yet warm and pleasant to the touch. It wipes clean with a damp cloth, never needs painting or refinishing, and comes in a wide variety of patterns and colors. It is unharmed by boiling water, most fruit juices, alcohol, oil, grease and ordinary household chemicals. It withstands heat up to 275° Fahrenheit and resists cigarette burns.

There are a number of good brands of laminated plastic surfacing, but only Consoweld Corporation produces its laminates on the basis of a scientific color system. Other manufacturers produce a variety of colors, but the colors are chosen in a subjective manner. In fact, Consoweld has adopted the color charts in this book as the basis of its color program.

Consoweld's patterns, too, are chosen on the basis of research with homemakers and homeowners. Thus, patterns that have deep meaning and lasting appeal for *people* are selected. If research shows that people react favorably to a design being considered, it is accepted. If tests show that the pattern does not have great appeal, it is rejected.

As a result, Consoweld includes a wide range of simulated woodgrains, marbles and fabrics, as well as abstract patterns and solid colors. The solid, vibrant colors are intended for commercial use. I do not recommend them. They are highly vibrant and could be emotionally disturbing in the home.

It is generally desirable, however, to have accessories such as lamps, cushions, canister sets, etc., in vibrant colors. The accents can be changed to more neutral tones if the color is found to be overstimulating. A permanent or long-life installation, such as a kitchen counter or a bathroom vanity counter, should be in a soft and soothing tone.

In describing furniture I express concepts but not actualities. The illustrations show various types of furniture, but specific furniture styles are not discussed. I merely point out general styles—Period versus Modern or Contemporary.

There are dozens of manufacturers of furniture and a great variety of designs of chairs, tables, buffets, sofas, etc. Some furniture makers operate with limited production schedules. They produce furniture like a sculptor produces bronzes, in a small number of copies. Outstanding among this type of furniture maker are Dunbar, Baker and Jamestown Royal.

There are also manufacturers who produce furniture pieces in great numbers. Mass production makes it possible for them to market high grade furniture at a low price. Kroehler is a good example of this type of manufacturer—and Kroehler promotes color. Kroehler sofas and chairs are available in high grade fabrics of nylon, cotton and wool, in a great variety of colors, in many neutral, delicate and rich tones.

Dunbar, Baker, Jamestown Royal and other exclusive furniture houses, as well as Kroehler, produce Modern or Contemporary furniture in wood, the traditional basic material. But new materials have made possible new types of furniture, too. Designers have used these materials to create furniture pieces with a totally new character.

The new furniture types embrace some significant psychological as well as social aspects. They are a break from tradition in materials and they promote a break from tradition in daily living.

This new type of furniture is in the realm of the casual, not formal; light, not heavy; colorful, not neutral; stimulating, not sedative. It promotes action as well as rest.

Many manufacturers produce casual furniture in aluminum and steel. This informal type of furniture is available for all places and all purposes: for the kitchen, recreation room, porch and patio; dining chairs, dining tables, coffee tables, settees, ottomans and chaise lounges. Ames Aire is one manufacturer that produces this type of informal, casual furniture which has characteristics that are possible only with modern materials.

The frames of all Ames Aire chairs and tables are made of zinc-coated tubular steel; seats and backs of the chairs are made of vinyl cord. Table tops are of tempered glass. Frames are rust-proof and the glass is impact and thermal resistant. The feet on all the pieces of furniture are made of nylon and are self-leveling. Although such furniture is light in weight, it is also durable and can take hard use outdoors as well as indoors.

This furniture is available in high preference colors. After reading the book you may decide you want a stimulating room; Ames Aire pieces in pink vinyl would be the answer. You may want a cooling sedative effect and choose a turquoise vinyl. You may want a feeling of sunshine and warmth and buy the furniture in yellow vinyl. If you still want your room to symbolize purity, you will choose white vinyl.

There are many makers of casual furniture in steel and in aluminum that give you a choice in color selection. Ames

Aire is particularly high in quality, durability and attractiveness, and had the highest ratings in a study of ten makes of casual, modern furniture.

Another line that had as high ratings in favorable associations, and just a little lower in preference ratings, was the line of Burke pedestal tables, chairs and stools made of cast aluminum and plastic. The Burke pieces are round, symmetrical and solid in appearance, and they are wholly modern in effect. The chairs are comfortable to the eye, clean looking and elegant. They are substantial in construction and appear substantial to the eye. They are conducive to relaxation visually.

The Burke tables with round tops on round pedestals are most attractive, and are practical because the tops are of laminated plastic.

For some rooms, you may wish to combine such different types of pieces as Ames Aire and Burke to produce a varied and pleasing effect. I have found the combination of Ames Aire and Burke pieces pleasing to the eye, and research showed that the combination was pleasing to most people.

One item not usually considered in a discussion of color in the home is the door. Few homemakers think of doors when they are planning their color schemes. Yet the door can be much more than a mere physical barrier. It can be endowed with psychological significance.

Even physically, a door can be different from the common image of a door. Traditionally, we think of the swinging door. Yet the swinging door is not the most practical kind of door, nor does it provide the greatest aesthetic possibilities.

A sliding door, one that slides into the wall, is much more practical than a swinging door because it does not consume space. It makes possible more practical and more attractive furniture arrangement.

There are two negative aspects about sliding doors. They cannot be put into existing houses or apartments, and in new housing construction they are more costly than swinging doors. But swinging doors can be eliminated by using *folding* doors. Most folding doors are made of a heavy fabric on a flexible steel frame; some are made of wood slats.

The fabric doors are more practical and modern, and for interior decor they offer more possibilities than wood doors. They are more practical because they are more durable than the wooden slats. They do not need finishing, are easy to clean with ordinary cleansers or soap and are not marred by impact of blunt objects. They are made of modern materials and can be tuned to the decor of the room.

In the past, the door was not related to any other part of the house. It was not like the wall. It was not like the windows. The folding door can be made to harmonize either with the wall or with the windows. It can be used between living room and hall, between kitchen and utility room, between dining area and living room, for closets and for the basement doorway.

Original ideas and unusual effects are possible with folding doors. For example, you can choose a fabric with a wood grain and a specific wood color. You can harmonize or match it with draperies so that the doorway and the windows have a unified effect. You can match it to the color of the walls, treat it like a mural or picture or give it the character of a tapestry or screen.

The folding door made of fabric is truly a product of modern industry that is in keeping with modern needs and in harmony with present day living. It saves space—an important factor in small apartments and in most houses. It is economical—the original investment is not great and the up-keep is least costly. It provides maximum psychological satisfactions—it can be made to harmonize with walls or windows and can serve aesthetically as a work of art, either in the form of a realistic picture with a window effect, an abstract design or an over-all pattern. It correlates with modern home furnishings in character, in texture as well as in color, in appearance as well as in flexibility.

In a study of folding doors, we found that the Modernfold door was the best of five brands of folding doors examined. The Modernfold door line has the greatest variety in color and texture, and is the best of the five brands in construction and operating efficiency.

Types of folding doors available are still limited, but Modernfold doors come in a number of high preference colors and in several fabric, texture-like patterns. Perhaps in the future an enterprising folding door manufacturer will market a number of pictorial and abstract designs, thus making it possible for the homemaker to enrich her home aesthetically with originality.

HOW TO COLOR-TUNE YOUR HOME

CHAPTER ONE

The Colors in Your Home Have Power

1. Why This Book

This is a book on color * as it applies to your home.

Superficially, it may seem that your home provides purely physical comfort. Actually, the home plays a vital psychological role. It is a primary factor in your emotional life and at the same time an expression of your character and individuality.

Your personality expresses itself in your choice of colors

---

* For details on the proper use of the color charts in the rear of the book, read pages 143 to 150.

1

for the walls, in your choice of the style of furniture and its arrangement. At the same time, the choices you have made continue to impress themselves on your personality and to influence you more and more as the years pass. Thus, the nature of your living space becomes intimately associated with you. It gradually becomes part of you and you a part of it.

A wild animal chooses its environment instinctively. Man does not. You are more likely to choose your environment for psychological, economic and social reasons which have obscured your self-preservative instincts. The environment that you have chosen for yourself "of your own free will" may do you much harm. It may be responsible for much unhappiness, which may be attributed to a totally different source.

There are deep-seated psychological factors that may make one "enjoy" suffering, that is, cause one to seek objects and create situations that will bring pain. For example, you may need and want more comfortable furniture and hope soon to be able to replace at least the old "stuffed" chair. When you are able to do so, you buy a period piece with a carved back and hard armrests. After using this chair for a few weeks you decide that it is no more comfortable than the one that you gave away or sold.

You ask yourself why you did it; you can't understand what made you buy *this* chair. Psychoanalytical studies tell us that we do such things because of deep-seated emotional drives. Deep in the unconscious, you may have associated the chair with happy days in your childhood or even with a glorious imaginary experience derived from reading a fairy tale. More about that in a later section.

Emotionally, you may need to surround yourself with

stimulating colors, yet you repeatedly choose cold and drab tones. You do this because Mrs. Jones has similar colors or because they are fashionable. That is, you *think* those are the reasons that cause you to choose them. It may well be that your choice has a much deeper psychological significance. This book will guide you in learning about yourself in relation to color.

You tell your "decorator" that you would like to have a "forest green" wall "just like the color in this magazine clipping." Then, after he laboriously mixes the color, you decide you don't like it or you say the match isn't right. (Even if the match is right, the color of the mixed paint cannot look exactly the same as on a printed page.) What may be happening is that you are having an inner conflict. You want to be in fashion, as prescribed by the magazine clipping, but some hidden emotional reaction combats this dictate of fashion.

Perhaps when you were a little girl you were lost in a forest. You were terribly frightened. Deep in the unconscious, you associate this green with that experience. What is recalled is not the traumatic experience in its entirety but only that part of it—the image of the color sensation—which is evoked by the color before your eyes. In a later section there will be more about this.

We can master our irrational emotional reactions only by uncovering their roots, by understanding their nature and origin. We can eliminate the unpleasant feelings caused by our internal conflicts only by first getting knowledge about ourselves. In this book I shall consider the psychological aspects of the home's physical environment and the full importance of the effects which surroundings, particularly in their color aspects, have on one's emotional stability.

Between these covers are reported the results of experiments conducted with colors at the Color Research Institute, excerpts from case histories demonstrating the psychological power of color and information gathered from various other studies. Pertinent aspects of human behavior patterns are covered, and some typical emotional reactions to color are described and analyzed.

A discussion of scientific principles and of case histories taken from Color Research Institute files was included in a previous book.[1] In that book, addressed primarily to the family provider, I demonstrated how we can use colors, images and patterns to increase profits in marketing. In an earlier book [2] I included general information gathered by Color Research Institute and treated color broadly in all its aspects; in a still earlier publication [3] I discussed design principles as aspects of everyday life. This book is for you, the homemaker, the promoter of domestic values—key to family happiness. After reading this book you will want to examine your home environment and analyze each room in the light of the information brought to you in these pages.

2. Color Study Is New

Perhaps in the past you wanted to learn about the nature of color. You may have heard something interesting about color or you may have been thinking of decorating a room. Here is a report about one intelligent woman who wanted to get information about color. We'll call her Mrs. X.

She went to the bookstore to get a book on the subject. The clerk suggested a book written by a famous artist whose work is noted for its color and pointed out that the

---

[1] *Color for Profit* (New York: Liveright Publishing Corp., 1951).

[2] *Colors: What They Can Do For You* (New York: Liveright Publishing Corp., 1947).

[3] *Living With Art* (Chicago: Kroch & Son, 1940).

book gave the fundamentals of color. Mrs. X was interested in basic information because she had had little art or color training.

The book contained a number of vibrant illustrations, and the artist-author told how he produced his rainbow effects with six basic colors. Mrs. X was fascinated with the book and decided to go further with the study of this subject.

A friend told her about another book on color. She lost no time in ordering it. From the second book she learned for the first time about the primary colors—red, blue and yellow. The author, who was a noted commercial artist, explained that all the illustrations in the book were produced with the three primary colors and black. He pointed out that all colors are derived from red, blue and yellow.

She told about her discovery of the color primaries to a couple who were her guests. The man was a high-school science teacher. He smiled indulgently and politely informed her that the primary colors are red, blue and green. The hostess produced her book. But the science teacher assured her that although artists use color they are not authorities on its scientific aspects.

Mrs. X later received a book from a friend in which she read that the great physicist Newton discovered seven colors in light and that all colors are in light, that light and color are the same thing.

Mrs. X discussed these puzzling bits of information when she was visiting her physician. The doctor gave her a book on optics that contained a chapter on color. He suggested that she read it. After finishing with this treatise she was more confused than ever. The author pointed out and gave evidence that there are four primary colors—red, green, blue and yellow.

The fact is that not much useful information on color

has been available to the homemaker, partly because books on the subject are primarily addressed to specialists in restricted scientific fields and partly because color research is comparatively new. Study of the psychological aspects of color is a particularly recent development.

Also, semantic difficulty or linguistic confusion is responsible for a great deal of misunderstanding about color. For example, the color that the scientist calls blue, the artist calls violet, and the scientist's red is the artist's orange.

The primary purposes of this book are to shed light on the nature of color as it affects everyday life and to give you practical guidance in color-tuning your living space. At the end of this book I clarify the seeming contradictions encountered by Mrs. X.

3. Color Is Not A Frill

The first characteristic that attracts you when you see an animal, object or place is its color. Color is experienced as a basic, primary sensation. Infants can distinguish primary colors before they can see simple geometric forms.

If you have normal eyes, you cannot avoid seeing and responding to the colors around you. There is no such thing as absence of color. Color is always present when your eyes are open—good color or bad color, inspiring or depressing, but color nonetheless.

You can shut off the radio or television set, but you can't "shut off" the colors in your home. Yet the colors may be greater irritants than any possible combination of sounds. You cannot shut off your visible environment; whether you are conscious of it or not, your environment has a great effect on your emotional stability.

Your surroundings may be inspiring or dispiriting. They

are never neutral in their effect. The colors around you influence your emotions, your attitudes and your behavior patterns, but most likely you don't know it. Unfortunately, emotional disturbances caused by wrong colors are rarely traced to the source. Many things are blamed for nervousness or a bad mood but the guilty colors hardly ever.

Some people imagine that they are detached from their environment. They have no idea that colors influence their temperaments and have effects on their efficiency and emotional stability. Others instinctively feel that there is some mysterious power in color, but they cannot comprehend its significance. Unfortunately, those who are aware of the value of appropriate color surroundings often turn for guidance to unreliable sources.

You may want the apartment redecorated because you feel that something is wrong with the color scheme—but you don't know what. You call in an interior decorator. He is usually an artist trained in designing interiors, but he may not be an expert in optics, the nature of light and the psychological effects of color. If he is not versed in these subjects, he may recommend a color scheme based upon such extraneous considerations as the following:

"These are the most fashionable colors this season."

"Mrs. Jones, the society leader, has a color scheme exactly like this."

"Aren't these stunning combinations?"

"Here are genuine Picasso colors."

The trouble with these suggestions is that they treat color as a whim, as a superficiality. After a consultation of this kind, you are likely to be more confused about color than ever.

The word "decorating" is somewhat unfortunate in that

it conveys the notion of frills and fads. It suggests a surface veneer, a superfluous luxury. It implies a lack of function, an absence of real purpose. It is used to represent conspicuous, useless consumption, and too often the display is really conspicuous and worse than useless in that it is emotionally upsetting.

Whoever said "Those who follow fashion blindly have no taste" hit the nail on the head. A housewife may be told that "last year it was fashionable to have light-colored walls and deep-colored carpets, but this year it is fashionable to have deep-colored walls and light-colored carpets." Or she may be assured that red and chartreuse were in style last year, while to be in style this year she will have to get green and burnt orange. Such nonsense makes people needlessly spend money (which perhaps is not serious if they have plenty of it) but may very well do much harm to home life.

I am looking forward to the day when color will not be linked with "decoration" but with design—when color for the home will be considered interior design and associated with the psychological make-up of the occupants. Either color must be taken away from the "decorator," or the "decorator" must become a student of psychology.

Home furnishers, the serious ones, will soon become aware of the psychological aspects of color. A noted Chicago dealer in home furnishings has cooperated with me and provided facilities in his business establishment for conducting psychological tests with colors. After witnessing the results, he adopted the scientific principles presented here and is now using them in serving his clients. In explaining some of the reasons for his success, he reports the following:

"Now, not only do I give my customers quality furniture with beautiful colors, but I have a reason for recommending each color; my customer has a reason for accepting each color, and my customers and I have reasons for combining specific colors. My customers are elated. They thank me profusely for what I have done for them. I am pleased and happy because I found the man who took the mystery out of color."

I appreciate the last part of his enthusiastic statement, but what he really meant, you and I can both conclude, is that by using sound principles of color in home furnishings he is assured of satisfied customers and an increasingly successful business. As he emphasized on another occasion, "My customers not only get harmonious colors for their homes, but they know why each color is chosen."

Taking the time to read this book is not a great price to pay for learning about the nature of color, its power and how to use it in your home, both for your own emotional needs and for the psychological benefit to your family. Here is abundant evidence that the colors of the furnishings in your rooms are not frills but vital psychological factors in your home and important elements in your emotional life.

This book will help you to explore your fundamental needs with regard to the world of color all around you. It will provide you with the facts you need to know in order to understand your emotional reactions to color. Finally, it is designed to show you how to surround yourself and your family with the colors that will add in no small measure to the enjoyment of your home.

4. An Experiment With Four Colors

The experiments and activities described below show something of the importance of color in everyday life. I make no attempt to be scientifically exhaustive, nor do I believe that you will be particularly concerned with knowing minute technical details. All I wish to do is to paint this truth in broad strokes: *color can have an extraordinary impact upon human emotions and well-being.* Let us briefly review some recorded experiments that illustrate this fact.

Four small rooms were color-treated: one entirely in red, the second in green, the third in blue and the fourth in yellow. In each room, walls and all furnishings—desks, chairs, typewriters—were the same respective color throughout.

The brilliant red color caused persons staying in the room to experience an increase in blood pressure and pulse. It was not possible for them to work in it or even to remain in it for any length of time. Normal activity was out of the question because of the overstimulation caused by the vibrant red.

The blue room produced the opposite effect. Blood pressure and pulse declined. The occupants became sluggish, and their rates of activity dropped below customary levels.

The brilliant yellow room caused no changes in blood pressure, but many activities were impossible because of extreme eyestrain.

The green-room experiment indicated that if any of these four hues can be called a "normal" color it is green. Although the occupants of the completely green room complained of monotony and asked for a varied color scheme, there was no evidence of any abnormal reaction. However, even the verbal reactions to the green room had some meaning because they showed that people object to color monotony and want a varied diet in color just as they do in food.

The experiment with green was carried further. A second

room was treated with three values * of green and a third room with three values of green and one tone of a complementary wine-red.

Free-association tests conducted in connection with these three rooms were quite revealing. Associations with the room of the single pure green hue were negative—that is, the uniformity apparently gave rise to some uncomfortable reactions.

Associations with the room that was treated in three values of green (a pure hue, a very deep tone and a delicate tint) were generally neutral. Few associations were either favorable or unfavorable.

But of the associations with the room of three values of green and a complementary color, 94 per cent were favorable. In other words, most people liked the room in which complementary colors were used.

5. We Eat With Our Eyes

Color plays a great part in the enjoyment of food, for the appetite is conditioned by the sense of sight just as much as by the sense of smell. The freshness of food is judged both by smell and color, and the enjoyment of food is governed by the colors on the dinner table as well as by the quality of the food and the ingenuity of the cook.

Several dinner and luncheon parties were given by a lighting engineer and by Color Research Institute to demonstrate that color does not affect merely the sense of sight but is closely related to the other senses as well and has a strong influence on our health.

On the dining table when the guests took their seats were

* For definitions of hue, tint, shade and tone, see pages 143 to 144.

dishes containing the finest and most appetizing-looking foods. When the lighting was switched from white to colored lights, the meat took on a dark gray color; the potatoes turned orchid. Salads were changed into muddy violet; the green peas looked like black caviar; the cream and the bread became blue, the coffee a sickly gray.

Most of the guests lost their appetites and could not eat. Those who forced themselves to consume the food became ill. In short, the dinners and luncheons were failures although the experiments were successful. They demonstrated that color has real power on emotions which in turn affect the digestive system.

6. Color With a Purpose

Often we speak of somber colors and gay colors, of colors that depress and colors that give pleasure. We have gone to places that made us feel gloomy and have been in places that inspired gaiety. However, we are rarely aware that the colors of a room may be largely responsible for the mood.

A manufacturer redecorated the lunchroom in his factory, changing the walls from a peach color to a light blue. The employees began to complain that it was chilly and that they had to wear their coats to lunch. The plant engineer knew that the temperature, which was thermostatically controlled, had not changed. A color specialist recommended that the walls be repainted peach and that orange slip covers be placed on the chairs. When warm colors replaced blue, complaints ceased. This is an excellent example of the psychological effect of color on an unconscious level, since the employees were not aware that the sense of coldness was caused by the blue color.

It is reported that a football coach used color in fitting

up his team's dressing rooms. For the room in which they lounged and relaxed, he chose a soft, restful blue; for the one in which "pep sessions" were held, a stimulating red. This is an example of how color can be used to achieve a definite objective.

An interesting report is that of a factory where merchandise packed in black boxes was loaded into cars. The workers showed fatigue in the early afternoon and frequently reported illness. A color specialist visited the plant and suggested painting the boxes a light green. After this was done complaints and absenteeism were reduced. The same principle applies to housework.

In another instance a well-known hostess was searching for an idea for an interesting party. A color specialist told her he could prescribe something that would assure her a most successful evening, provided that she served no alcoholic drinks the first two hours. Somewhat skeptically she agreed to follow his instructions and put magenta light bulbs in every fixture in the house, placing a number of them even under the furniture.

Though the drinks were not served at all, the party was a great success. The hostess noted that husbands were especially attentive to their wives and wives to their husbands. The reason, in all probability, was that magenta red is flattering to the complexion and is a color of high preference.

Perhaps some magenta in your home can make a major contribution.

7. Emotional Problems and Color

A mother pointed out a policeman to her little boy, foolishly telling him that if he did not behave, this man would take him away and lock him up in jail.

Soon afterward the boy's father bought a new blue worsted suit for himself. Thereafter, the boy became highly agitated whenever he saw his father in the new suit.

However, the relationship between the father's blue suit and the child's abnormal behavior was not discovered by the parents. Only much professional psychoanalytical probing revealed that the little boy associated the blue suit with the man who was going to take him to jail. The color, in this case, was a stronger emotional factor than the father-son relationship. (It is, of course, evident here that the father-son relationship was not very close.) The impression from such an experience, had it not been detected and corrected, could have resulted in a strong, lifelong dislike for blue.

Here is another significant case:

Jerry was six years old when his mother brought him to a children's psychiatric clinic. The mother reported that Jerry not only refused to go to school but would get sudden fits whenever school was mentioned.

The mother was advised by the interviewer to matriculate the boy in the special classes for children conducted by the clinic. In these classes the children are observed by trained psychiatric social workers, and a daily record is kept of each child's behavior.

The first two days Jerry was inhibited, fearful and unexpressive but otherwise normal. On the third day he became hysterical and again on the fourth day.

An analysis of the daily record showed that the hysteria took place each time during an art session. The connection between the hysterical behavior and the art class appeared to be coincidental until all the minute elements of the art class had been classified and analyzed.

The psychiatric social worker found something that would have been meaningless to the average teacher. She observed that the hysteria took place only when the children were painting with orange paint. They painted with red tempera on Monday, with blue on Tuesday and with orange on Wednesday.

For some reason, either planned or coincidental, the same orange paint was used again on Thursday; again on Thursday, as on Wednesday, Jerry was hysterical. On Friday the class painted with yellow, and although the boy was highly nervous, he carried through his art activity without incident. The second week and the third week confirmed the correlation between the orange color and the six-year-old's hysterical behavior.

Finally the boy was placed with a group of children who worked with all colors except orange and colors closely related to orange. No hysteria developed.

During the time the boy was attending the classes, another psychiatric social worker was meeting the boy's mother twice a week. When the correlation of the orange color and the boy's hysteria was made known to the mother's social worker, she began to ask the mother leading questions. Previously the mother had described her child's hysterical behavior as coming on suddenly, with no assignable cause whatever. Now the following story came out.

The mother and her son had been visiting relatives in another state when school began. Jerry, therefore, did not start school at the same time as the other boys and girls. When he was brought to school by his mother for the first time it was just before Halloween. The class was given a project of drawing a pumpkin.

Because it was Jerry's first experience with tempera he

was timid about handling it, and when the class session was over his pumpkin drawing was not finished.

The teacher was one of those who believe in enforcing rigid discipline. She announced that all who had not finished the drawing lesson must remain after class to finish it. Jerry watched the boys and girls rush out of the room to meet their mothers in the foyer. He alone had to remain to finish drawing the pumpkin.

The large classroom suddenly became unnaturally quiet. He saw that he was alone with the grim teacher sitting at her desk on a high platform very distant from him. He became terrified and began to cry. The teacher descended upon him and reprimanded him in a harsh voice that echoed through the large, empty room. The boy became hysterical, and the teacher dragged him out to his mother with the exclamation that he was a very bad boy, lazy and troublesome. This traumatic experience became associated in the boy's unconscious with the color of pumpkin—orange.

Had this association of orange with a traumatic experience not been discovered and corrected in the child, the boy could have grown up with a color complex that might have been a handicap throughout his adult life. There are many adults who have strong color phobias, due to similar childhood traumatic experiences associated with colors.

The cases outlined below illustrate some of the more serious psychological difficulties that can be aggravated if not created by the "wrong" colors.

An unhappy-looking man told a color specialist, whom he knew from schooldays, that his wife was suffering from the "blues," that she had hardly talked to him for months and had been consistently morose. He thought perhaps a visit from an old friend might do her some good.

The visit was uneventful. The young wife served tea mechanically and answered inquiries politely. Otherwise, she did not utter a word. To the question of how she liked her apartment, she replied, "I hate it!" That was the only emotional response she made during the entire evening.

Upon the visitor's departure, the husband thanked him for coming, at the same time betraying disappointment that the friend's visit had failed to arouse the wife from her lethargy. If anything, the visitor seemed to have aggravated the situation with his constant questioning.

On the following day, the color specialist called his friend and emphatically advised him to redecorate the apartment and to purchase a few small accessories. He urged that the blue walls be changed to a warm tint or tone of red—peach or neutral orange. He insisted that all black objects be removed and that a number of pictures, ceramics and pieces of sculpture, predominantly red or orange, be added to the furnishings.

At first the young woman was indifferent to the alterations, but in a few days she began to take notice of the new regime. Within a month her interest deepened into enthusiasm, and she regained much of the vivacity of a normal, happy wife. This case is an excellent demonstration of the psychological power of colors. The blue-and-black environment, we have reason to believe, aggravated the woman's moodiness, while the change to red, which apparently stimulated her as nothing else had done for months, helped her toward normal behavior and happiness.

The following is a case in which red had an unfavorable effect. A young woman married a man who had a beautifully furnished apartment, which she had visited on numerous occasions during their engagement. Everything seemed in order except for one thing. The new husband had the formerly blue walls painted orange and had made red the dominant color. He wanted to surprise the lady—and he succeeded.

She had always been an overly excitable person, and the blazing color scheme did not help her to control her temperamental outbursts. Her erratic behavior was attributed to many causes. What is certain, however, is that a change back to blue walls was followed by the return of a more equable disposition.

The power of color was demonstrated again in the situation of a young wife who, with her husband, a veteran, lived in the only place they had found available, a drab shack which offered no possibilities for colorful decorating.

In spite of her happiness at being reunited with her husband, she became morose and complained of frequent abdominal pains for which her doctor could find no explanation. After five months of increasing melancholy, she found relief only after she became busily engaged in planning color for the new home she and her husband eventually found.

Here is another example of how color can either contribute to or alleviate emotional difficulties.

A young army officer, his wife and their child lived in a one-room apartment with camp-made furniture. One day when the baby was placed in a high chair, she began to scream loudly.

When the chair was examined, it was found that a nail had become exposed and had pierced deeply into the baby's flesh. Thereafter, though the parents made certain that there would be no repetition of this unfortunate experience, nothing seemed capable of inducing the child to sit again in the high chair.

The situation was explained to a friend who was a color specialist, and he suggested that they paint the red high chair green. After this was done, the child was perfectly content to sit in it. But it is highly probable that this baby girl will grow up with a marked prejudice against red.

We see from such typical incidents that a strong dislike for a color may be traced to a painful experience associated with that color in early life, as in the case of a woman who detests turquoise blue because an aunt who was cruel to her as a child was fond of green-blue (turquoise) garments.

We are generally not conscious of the colors around us. Most reactions to our environment remain in a state of mere sensation. We experience the sensations on an unconscious level, that is, we are usually completely unaware of them. Yet these sensations affect our emotions; they act for us or against us.

8. Visual Stimulants and Sedatives

Experiments and case histories reported on the preceding pages indicated that colors are divided into two general psychological classifications—stimulants and sedatives.

All red hues are stimulating to some degree. The warmer the red (the more yellow it contains), the more aggressive and advancing it is. A color is said to be "advancing" when it appears nearer to the eye than other colors lying in the same plane. Children, primitive peoples and the cultured and sophisticated alike are stimulated by red. Love of this color is widespread.

Yet there are some people who have a strong aversion to red. Such a reaction, as we have seen, often can be traced to some traumatic childhood experience associated with that color. Also, vibrant orange-red and other warm reds are rejected by certain cultural groups as being associated with overly strong feelings. However, a cool red such as magenta is readily acceptable to most people.

Blue, though the coldest of colors, also enjoys wide popularity. It is generally found that this color is a psychological sedative for people who are inclined to be easily overstimulated. It can be depressing for the morose type of individual, and persons inclined to melancholy should avoid an overabundance of it. Tests have shown that most people react more favorably to green-blue than they do to violet-blue.

Yellow produces the sensation of sunlight and warmth. The psychological reaction to yellow is not as positive as it is to red or blue, and the slightest change in yellow will increase or decrease its warmth. Hence it is a color that needs careful handling.

We are constantly surrounded by green, and because the color is unconsciously associated with food, nature and growth, it produces the most comfortable reactions. Blue-greens are cool and yellow-greens are warm, but even a cool green is not really a cold color. Blue-greens have very high preference. They are among the most popular colors.

Orange, on the other hand, has such warmth and vibrancy that in its pure state many people quickly tire of it because of its overstimulating effect.

Violet and purple, throughout history, have been used as symbols of dignity, authority and power. They are cold and austere colors. Violet and purple are not common colors in nature; rarity adds to their distinctiveness.

The warm and stimulating colors are yellow, yellow-green, orange, orange-red, red, brown, beige, buff and all other colors that are predominantly yellow or red in hue.

The cool and sedative colors are blue-green, green-blue, blue, violet-blue, violet, magenta red and all other colors that are predominantly blue in hue.

Primitive peoples have very strong emotional responses to color, but they are attracted by pure hues only. Delicate tints are "washouts" to them, and are probably thought of as representing weakness. Many savage tribes associate loud colors, no less than loud noises, with manliness and power.

The attraction to pure hues is, of course, not confined to savages. Civilized people, who are not inhibited or restricted by convention, show similar tendencies in moderation. European peasants, who have a tradition of their own, use rich colors to embroider their festive garments and to decorate their homes and household goods.

American farmers habitually paint their barns red—primarily because they unconsciously want to counteract the steady overdose of green to which they are exposed. In searching for a practical reason for using red paint, farmers generally say that they use it because it is not a costly paint. Actually, green oxide or yellow ochre is just as economical.

In cities, especially among the underprivileged, there is a considerable craving for pure hues. We can understand readily how rich, vibrant colors lend stimulation to people whose lives in the main are drab and monotonous.

Children from the age of one to six are very much intrigued with pure colors. Normally, they like red best and blue least; yellow, though it has greater visibility than red, fails to stimulate them. Like savages, they are not attracted by delicate tints or deep shades. Baby pink may thrill Mama, but it leaves baby unimpressed. A very strong red, on the other hand, may annoy the cultivated sensibilities of the modern mother, yet provide a distinct thrill for the two- or three-year-old.

In recent years some very significant studies have been made on the relationship of color preference to emotional stability and mental hygiene. Many more studies are needed before final conclusions can be drawn. However, it has been cbserved that children who are emotionally unstable or given to morbidity choose blue or black as their favorite color. Children who are starved for sunshine prefer yellow, and those in the slum areas where shrubbery is rare are attracted by green.

Normally, if you try giving a baby two identical toys—one red, the other blue—almost always the child will choose the red or stimulating one. If the contrary happens, there is likely to be a special reason. One such reason may be that the child once hurt himself with a red toy. The red color, being linked with pain, becomes unwelcome. Or the child may have been *taught* to associate hot objects with red by being given repeated warnings such as, "Don't touch it. It's red hot!" Then again, simply as a conventional symbol of danger, red often brings about an uncomfortable feeling. On the whole, though, and under normal circumstances, the average child will be drawn to the warm, vibrant colors of the red family.

One suspects that children react more vigorously to strong colors than most adults because they are less inhibited by the social taboos that condemn expression of natural feelings. With regard to the "humanizing" effect of a good color scheme—the role it can play in emotional fulfillment—we can learn much both from children and adults who have an unrestrained delight in color. Of course color may soothe or stimulate; the need is for a color diet that will provide the proper balance of emotional and aesthetic nutrients.

9. Bright or Muted Colors in Your Home?

Pure colors can be taken only in small doses. Experiments have indicated that a normal person couldn't live in a room painted all in red. Pure red in large doses is overstimulating. On the other hand, it would be depressing to spend long periods of time in a blue room. For walls, therefore, pure color is diluted with white or neutralized by being mixed with a small amount of its complementary color or with gray paint.

However, we should keep in mind that what is too small a dose for one person can be too great for another but just right for a third individual. Some people need as much stimulation as possible in their living quarters. Others should have a room with relaxing colors.

As has already been pointed out, bright colors and particularly reds appeal to children, to primitives and, in smaller doses, to adults who are not afraid to stimulate their emotions.

If you are unduly inhibited, if you are fearful of giving your emotions free play or if they are already overworked outside the home, if you are strait-laced about visual cocktails, if you are more concerned about maintaining an artificial decorum than developing a creative color sense—then you will avoid any suggestion of bright colors in your home.

Of course, you should never go to the other extreme of using nothing but bright colors. Vibrant hues in large doses, without eye-resting areas, can become a severe strain on the nervous system. And one of the primary functions of the modern home is to provide rooms in which the occupants can relax.

Gray is a neutral color. It neither advances nor recedes, is neither warm nor cold. It neither stimulates nor calms. It can therefore be used in combinations with a pure cool color or a pure warm color.

Tan contains a touch of orange-red, but is mostly gray. Peach consists of white and orange-red. Brown is a combination of black and orange-red. Such muted, warm, vibrant colors, which have been diluted with white or neutralized with gray, should be used with bright green-blues, although a brilliant burnt-orange piece of accent in the drapery or on a chair need not be avoided.

Normally, people feel most comfortable with combinations of diluted and bright colors, for example magenta red with a delicate or grayed green, or burnt orange with tan and green-blue (turquoise).

A gay interior may be achieved by use of a highly colorful sofa, some colorful chairs in complementary colors, a few bright pictures and some brilliant ceramics. Your wall will be a rich neutral (a gray that is not slate, but reddish, greenish, bluish or yellowish) and your rug a toned-down color. The rug may be complementary to the wall color.

Such a room will give you ample stimulation with sufficiently large areas in the rug and on the wall for optical relief. But here I have somewhat anticipated later portions of this book.

10. Every Color Has a Mate

Colors are components of light. Where there is no light there is no color. Objects generally absorb some of the light and reflect the rest of it. The color of the object is dependent upon which parts of light are absorbed and reflected. Thus a red object reflects the red part of the light. An object is black when it absorbs all the colors; it is white when it reflects them all.

Color harmony is functionally dependent upon the eye and in this sense is a physiological phenomenon. The eye is anatomically and physiologically equipped to receive the waves of white light and the waves of colors which are actually parts of white light.

The after-image phenomenon demonstrates the complementary relationships between red and green and between blue and yellow. Looking at one color brings forth an after-image of its complement. Place a small green object before you and a sheet of white paper nearby. Gaze at the green article for about a minute; then turn to the white paper; you will see on the white background the appearance of the same object in red. This is called an after-image. After looking at green-blue, if you turn your gaze to a white or neutral surface, you will see orange-red; after looking at magenta red, you will perceive green. And so with violet-blue and yellow and all other pairs of complementaries.

For reasons beyond our immediate concern every hue brings forth a complementary after-image.

When complementary colors are placed next to each other, the effect is both stimulating and pleasing because the after-image of one color enhances the other. The blue after-image from yellow enhances the blue and vice versa. The red after-image from green enhances the red and again vice versa.

Because of the after-image we can have harmonious combinations of a neutral color with a pure hue. Gray appears reddish next to green, yellowish next to blue and bluish next to yellow. The after-image on a gray surface is weaker than on a white surface because gray does not reflect as much light.

That the association of colors in pairs is a natural phenomenon of vision is corroborated by the facts of color blindness. Usually color blindness takes the form of inability to see red and green. Very occasionally the color-blind person cannot see blue and yellow. Total color blindness, incidentally, is rare.

Complementary colors are natural, physical pairs because when mixed in light they produce white light. They are optical pairs as demonstrated by the after-image. They are also a psychological balance of warm and cool hues. From a pair of complementaries you can get a host of shades, tints and tones, all of which comprise a family of colors that can be combined and tuned to stimulate, to relax and in general to provide pleasant home surroundings.

The physical, optical and psychological aspects of color are explained more fully in later pages.

11. Your Basic Color

First of all, find the color that is to dominate the room. This color should be determined primarily on a psychological basis. It should be a color that is psychologically beneficial to your emotional make-up. Keep in mind the general psychological classifications of colors:

Orange-red is a warm color that is highly stimulating. Peach, being a mixture of orange-red and white, also possesses a warm quality.

Green-blue (turquoise) is a cool color that provides a soothing background for high-strung persons.

Green is easy on the eyes. It is neither stimulating nor sedative in nature.

Magenta red is a cool red. It is mildly exotic and normally pleasing to most people.

Violet is cold and austere; for some people it is also exotic.

Yellow tinged with blue is greenish and cool but is usually regarded as too vibrant and too strong for general comfort.

Yellow tinged with red is warm but is also too vibrant and too strong to be used pure.

Keep in mind that dosage, or the quantitative element, is as important in color as it is in everything else. A small area of brilliant red may be pleasantly stimulating, but four red walls can be nerve-wracking.

Limiting the area covered by a hue is not the only method of reducing the color's effect. A similar aim is achieved when paint is mixed, by diluting a color with white or neutralizing it with gray. Thus, a mildly stimulating effect can be created in a room—either by painting the walls with peach, which is produced by mixing orange-red with white or light gray, or by combining orange-red objects or accessories with walls and floor coverings of a neutral color.

After you have selected the major color, let us say burnt orange for a sofa and a chair, the next step is to select colors to go with it. We now have a specific and scientifically established guide for our procedure. Physical and optical considerations as well as psychological needs suggest that the other colors in the room should be related and complementary to the burnt orange.

It follows, then, that the burnt orange should be accompanied by orange-red, peach, tan or brown (related colors) and by green-blue in light, medium and dark tones (complementaries). Two or more spots of pure green-blue (turquoise) in the drapery, pictures or ceramics will be effective.

Peach, as well as various browns and tans are based on orange-red, and dozens of shades, tints and tones are based on green-blue, all of which you can see on color charts No. 3 and No. 9.

Each hue has not only a mate but a family. The complementary hue is the mate, and the related values—shades, tints and tones of both hues are the family. Hundreds of colors can be made from one hue by mixing it with white and/or black. Each color chart in this book shows twenty-five colors made from one hue. This means that in any particular instance the charts will help you make a choice from fifty harmonious colors, all derived from a pair of complementary hues.

Related colors differ in lightness or darkness but not in hue. For example, brown is black with orange-red; tan is black and white with orange-red; peach is white with orange-red. Orange-red can be the basic hue of a hundred different shades, tints and tones.

Complementary colors are pleasing combinations because they complete each other. They provide an "eyefull." Continually to see only one color or a combination of noncomplementary colors leaves a gap in the perceptual process. That is why we don't feel satisfied with colors that are not combined in complementary sets.

Analogous color schemes are either overstimulating or depressing. For example, a color combination such as yellow, yellow-green and orange is much too aggressive, and one such as violet, violet-blue and blue is much too cold.

Color combinations of this kind are not only gaudy and in bad taste but are often emotionally upsetting.

This fact brings us directly to our next topic.

12. Balancing Your Color Diet

A mile of red soon ceases to be stimulating and becomes irritating. Maximum favorable color-power, as we have seen, depends on variety and contrast. Any one fundamental color is not enough for a person's needs, any more than the best bread or the finest cheese makes a balanced diet. Just as your food must be varied, so should your colors. The basic dish of color for your personality must have some salt and pepper.

A predominantly yellow room should have its spots of complementary violet-blue, a predominantly violet-blue room its accents of complementary yellow. In other words, if you are a highly irritable individual who feels most comfortable with blue, it does not follow that you should have nothing but blue in your room.

I have already pointed out that blue alone, instead of being soothing, becomes depressing. Normal people must have variety and stimulation in a blue room. For a similar reason, complementary red accents are important in a green room. Remember that by using complementary colors we follow optical and physical as well as psychological laws.

Small areas of a complementary cool color in the furnishings make a predominant warm color even more vibrating and brilliant. But these small spots of cool color have little psychological effect next to the predominating warm color.

Having a color scheme of two warm colors, such as orange and orange-red (or any of the various related tones of brown and tan derived from these) is not the way to balance your color diet. Orange and orange-red, deep brown, light brown and tan, all being warm colors, normally provide insufficient variety of psychological effect.

On the other hand, a pair of complementary hues provides the basis for a balanced and complete color scheme. For example, if your color scheme is predominantly pink (a derivative of red) with rich green accents, the other colors can be shades, tints or tones of red and of green. If you want to heighten the stimulating effect, pure red should be introduced.

Noncomplementary colors that are neutral in value, such as gray, beige, tan or the natural colors of wood, will not interfere with eye-ease. Noncomplementary colors in small spots, as in tweedy material or in some impressionist pictures, mix in the eye as gray. Large objects in rich colors that are noncomplementary, such as a blue chair in a red and green room, are definitely an optical strain and a psychological irritant.

There is no reason why you can't use more than a dozen colors based on one hue, meaning that you can have a dozen tones of green with as many or more tones of red. By employing a variety of colors, all of which are derived from complementary hues, you achieve an effect of both diversity and harmony.

The floor-covering or rug is an important factor in giving unity to an interior. A harmonious effect can be achieved by having a rug of the same hue as the walls, but contrasting in tone—a deep green rug with light green walls or light green rug with deep green walls. An equally harmonious and unified effect can be produced by having the rug complementary to the walls. This means, for example, that the rug may be of a tone or shade of orange (tan, beige, brown) for blue walls and of a tone or shade of red for green walls. A very light rug with dark furniture or a deep-colored rug with light furniture produces a dramatic effect which is pleasing to many people but too contrasting for some.

The furniture and walls should always be either complementary in hue or contrasting in tone. If a piece of furniture is complementary in hue to the background, contrast in tone is not always essential. But if furniture and walls are the same in hue, contrast in tone is needed, that is, dark furniture should go with light walls and light furniture with a deep-toned background.

13. Color, Illumination and Temperature

Hues, shades, tints and tones * all reflect some of the lighting in the room. Of the pure hues, yellow reflects the most light, about 75 per cent of the illumination, and blue the least, about 5 per cent. Shades generally reflect from 3 to about 8 per cent, tones 20 to 40 per cent and tints from 60 to 80 per cent, of the light striking them.

The darker the color, the more light it absorbs; the lighter the color, the more light it reflects. Therefore, the color value or specific tone of the surfaces is an important factor in all interiors where illumination is a problem.

Furniture, as well as walls, ceiling and floor, is a factor in lighting. Where proper lighting cannot be obtained by providing an additional light source, illumination can be increased by making the surfaces of the interior lighter in color.

In the case of a ceiling that is not within the line of vision, white should be used because it will reflect 10 to 15 per cent more light than even a delicate tint will.

However, if essential lighting can be provided by merely adding natural or artificial illumination, you should disregard the light-reflection factor of the color and consider only the psychological aspects.

* See pages 143 to 144 for full discussion of these terms.

Since light and heat are both derived from the sun, the relationship of color to temperature is evident. Because a white object reflects light it also reflects heat. Black absorbs light and therefore absorbs heat.

When Piccard went up into the stratosphere in a black gondola, the temperature outside the gondola registered 75° F. below zero, while the temperature inside the gondola was 100° F. above zero. On his second flight into the stratosphere he used a white gondola, with the result that the inside temperature dropped below the freezing point.

Profiting from Piccard's experience, Fordney and Settle went up in a gondola painted half white and half black. A sufficient amount of heat was absorbed by the black part to keep the average inside temperature fairly comfortable.

Members of a polar expedition kept their drinking water from freezing by painting the bags black. During the day these bags absorbed enough heat from the sun to raise the temperature of the water to 60° F. when the outside air was 20° F. below zero.

In another incident of this type, half of each side of a cottage in the mountains was painted white and the other part black. The white parts gathered a thick coat of ice while the black remained clear for some time.

Perhaps the most dramatic (and gruesome) illustration of how colors absorb and reflect heat was furnished by a report from Hiroshima after the atomic bomb explosion. Burned into the flesh of those victims who had worn clothing of various colors were the imprints of the designs. Deep colors permitted very deep burns while lighter tones prevented all but surface burns. Where the delicately tinted parts of the designs covered the body there were few or no burns. It is worth knowing that even the terrific radiation from an atomic blast can be repelled by white or delicately colored garments.

In short, color is physically as well as psychologically cool or warm. If yours is a problem of getting sufficient heat, remember that the lighter the color on the walls the more heat as well as light will be reflected into the interior. But always bear in mind that the psychological power of color is more important to you than its absorption or reflection of heat and light.

14. The Over-All Picture in Choosing Colors

Since masses of pure hues are either overstimulating or depressing, you should choose diluted or neutralized colors for the large areas in your home, such as walls and floors. Then, if the colors are warm they will be energizing instead of irritating, and if they are cool they will be relaxing instead of depressing.

Keep in mind the facts about light reflection. If you want your room to be light you will choose light tints. You know that a deep tone may give the room distinction but it will also absorb light.

Another point to consider is the kind of natural light you have. It is not generally advisable to have blue predominate in a room that has only northern exposure. Because north light contains much blue, it is cold and should not be combined with blue surface color. And it is not generally beneficial to have yellow or peach as the major color in a room in which there is abundant sunlight, because direct sunlight makes such a color too warm and too vibrant.

You should know that deep tones advance and make a room look smaller, whereas light tints recede and lend spaciousness to an interior. Red is more advancing than blue, and thus a red-tinted room seems smaller than a blue-tinted room.

Don't forget the purpose of a room. For your bedroom, you may want colors that are soft and relaxing. In your living room, on the other hand, you may wish to have somewhat gayer and more contrasting color values that are conducive to activity.

Some brilliant colors should go into baby's room. They should be distinct primaries, and red objects should predominate. Unfortunately, most mothers are not aware that delicate pinks and pastel blues are meaningless to baby and that brilliant red gives the greatest thrill to the tot. But now you know.

You recognize, of course, that the most important factor of all in planning colors for your home is the psychological one. If you are of a nervous disposition, predominantly cool colors are likely to be beneficial for you. If you suffer from frequent periods of melancholy, by all means surround yourself with an abundance of colors that are warm and stimulating. If you are emotionally stable, it is possible for you to have as many shades, tints and tones as you wish, both cool and warm, although even then either the warm or the cool colors should prevail.

Whichever color you prefer, you will make sure that the room has accents of the complementary hue. A predominantly violet-blue room should have yellow accents; a yellow room should be given violet-blue accents; a pink room should be accented with green; a room in green tints and tones should be embellished with red accents.

The accents will be in pictures, drapery patterns, furniture upholstery, sculpture pieces, vases, lamp shades and ceramics. And you will realize that although the accents of complementary hue should predominate, small spots of other hues need not be excluded from the setting.

It may be noted at this point that pictures provide effective accents, because their distribution over the room can be controlled and because they can incorporate not only complementary accents but colors related to the setting. They also provide additional aesthetic and cultural values.

In summary: Select the specific colors which meet your psychological needs or those of the member of the family who is to be the occupant of the room, and take into consideration the lighting and proportional and dimensional aspects of the interior at the same time.

15. Gray for Balance and Harmony

Much modern furniture has a light-colored finish. Generally, the yellow of the wood is sufficiently toned down not to interfere with a green and magenta-red color scheme. Also, the grain of the wood softens the yellow considerably.

However, if you find that the yellow in your large pieces of wood furniture is too vibrant and you know you should have a green and red setting, you can have these colors in combination with neutral gray walls and/or rug, which will take on a violetish tinge next to the toned yellow wood, a greenish tinge next to the red articles and a reddish tinge next to the green objects in the room.

If you have had experience with color, you may have found that when small amounts of totally different colors are mixed with grays (black and white) the mixtures look almost alike. For example, gray plus some magenta red appears to the eye very much like gray plus some violet-blue. (See Color Charts.)

You can therefore have a violet-gray or magenta-gray in

combination with magenta red, green and a soft-toned yellow, such as in light or natural wood. The magenta-gray or violet-gray is related to the magenta red and complements both the soft yellow and the green. In other words, the gray color serves a dual purpose: it provides a blending background for the magenta red, and it absorbs the after-image color from both the toned yellow and the green. We thus get an effect of balance and harmony.

A color scheme based on green-blue and orange-red may also be combined with a yellow, which is no brighter than the color of light finished wood, by using a perfectly gray neutral background or a gray having a tinge either of the orange-red or the green-blue. In juxtaposition with the light yellow wood, a turquoise blue-gray wall or rug will look slightly violetish because the violet after-image of the yellow will be added to the blue. A tan (gray plus orange-red) wall will appear cooler in juxtaposition with the light yellow wood pieces because the violet after-image will be added to the tan.

In a yellow and violet-blue interior plan the light yellow wood is, of course, related to the yellow and complementary to the violet-blue. Gray is not needed here as a device for balancing and harmonizing near-neutral, noncomplementary colors. However, even here you will want moderately neutral colors in at least some of the large areas to avoid an overabundance of pure hues and their usual consequences of optical irritation and emotional disturbance. You will want the violet-blue diluted and the yellow toned down considerably.

A room based on violet-blue and yellow should have its rug and/or walls of violet-gray, tan or beige. Perhaps also some of the furniture pieces could be tones derived from violet-blue and yellow. However, some spots should be brilliant yellow and others pure violet-blue to provide stimulating, vivid and exotic accents.

Always keep in mind that no matter on which set of complementary hues you base your color scheme, the type of lighting affects surface color. A large window on the north side makes gray or white seem bluish. Western light gives warmth to a neutral or cool color. The color remains comparatively constant on a wall that is exposed only to a north window. The color changes radically hour by hour on a wall exposed to the east or west.

16. Composing Your Living Space

The right colors are not all you need in getting the most out of a room. The arrangement of the furniture is important, and so is the style or character of the furniture pieces a vital factor in planning your living space.

In arranging your room you will, of course, be conscious of the need for freedom of movement. At the same time you should keep in mind that when arranging a room you are very much like an artist composing a picture. You deal with minor and major objects (forms). You deal with minor and dominant colors, with neutral colors and color accents. You have a variety of objects which you must harmonize in order to give the room an effect of unity.

Composition is the art of organization, of arranging and bringing diverse elements into order and unity. Any interior containing more than one element must be composed in order to be functional or pleasing.

The proportions and dimensions of the pieces of furniture, the relative intensity and relative tonality of the colors, decide the character of a living space as they do of a pictorial composition. A pleasing composition has variety that is in harmony, an effect of movement that is in unity. Variety, harmony, movement and unity are present in some degree in every composition, whether it is pictorial or a living space.

In relation to psychological effect, I suggest classification into four major types of composition or arrangement:

1. Dramatic: a maximum of contrast with abrupt transitions of value and hue.
2. Lyrical: a maximum of delicate gradations.
3. Static: a maximum of parallelism and symmetrical or formal balance.
4. Passive: a maximum of repetition and continuity, "overall" pattern.

In a dramatic arrangement, there are extremely contrasting forms and colors. Angles are next to curves. Sharp lights are set against deep shadows. Vibrant colors are opposed to deep shades.

A lyrical arrangement has a delicate effect. It is never turbulent. It ripples but never roars. It moves but does not leap. Its forms, lines and colors have limited variety. The colors are delicate and merge softly.

Static arrangement is dignified, formal. Balanced but lacking in variety, it is devoid of an effect of movement and is not stimulating. Although it may arouse interest, it does not intrigue, and the interest is not lasting. Its symmetry produces an effect of form at rest and of solidity, both of which are important characteristics of the architectural design of a large structure. The function of a structure is to be at rest; therefore, symmetry is a functional quality in a building. In a room, static, symmetrical arrangement of furniture is hardly conducive to activity. It is more conducive to boredom.

Passive arrangement is on a two-dimensional plane and serves as a background. The repetition of a soft, simple design is quietly pleasing and soothing. A curved soft line is passive. It guides the eye unobtrusively, hardly making you conscious of its presence, yet producing a pleasant sensation. The effect of a passive design or arrangement is psychologically similar to the sensation one has in listening to the waves of a large body of water washing rhythmically against a sandy shore. Repetition is the main element of the over-all pattern as it is of the movement of the sea. In a passive design or arrangement, the basic unit may be lyrical in character, but the rest of the units are a repetition of the first. Thus, the active stimulus is the same as if there were only one unit; the one unit (object) stimulates, the rest leaves you unaroused, yet pleased by the continuous repetition of the original sensation.

For a successful room arrangement it is best to combine dramatic or lyrical elements with passive elements. The room may have one static, symmetrical wall, but to arrange the entire room in a static or symmetrical manner is to court boredom. Equally tedious is to combine static arrangement with passive pattern.

17. In the Hands of the "Experts"

In what follows, I don't want to be understood as saying that there are no competent decorators nor honest tradesmen. I merely wish to put you on guard against some of the pitfalls that may handicap your homemaking career.

Imagine that you are moving into a new house or apartment without having read thus far in the present book. You plan to buy furniture and accessories and see to the "decorating" of the new home.

First of all, you must consider what to put upon the

walls. You thought you always knew; now you are beset by doubts. You go for guidance to a hardware store, a paint shop or an interior decorating studio.

Possibly you may get some real help. And even if you encounter people who may not have your best interests at heart, you can't quite imagine yourself giving in to them too easily. Too often, however, you are swayed in spite of yourself, and the story unwinds about as follows.

The "expert" looks you over and perhaps decides that you have some money to spend. He begins to give you service with the aid of phrases such as "fine quality," "in fashion" or "so-and-so says it's best."

You are looking at the paint swatches. You think you'd like a delicate blue-gray for your living-room walls because you believe your fine pictures will show up well against that color. But you are not sure. You hesitate to say so. The "expert" is talking. You don't want to interrupt.

Because he happens to be out of that color or because there is not much profit in your choice, he tells you that it is not a "good" color, that a lady of your social position should have a more fashionable color, such as forest green. The deep, blackish green "is the color favored by the people living on the hill." He is an "expert," and he sells to these people. He ought to know what is best. You are not convinced that your own original choice was right so you get the black-green paint for your living room.

You are pressured in a similar manner into getting a chocolate brown for the master bedroom. To simplify the problem, you decide to use the same color for the other bedrooms. For your bathroom, you are encouraged to choose blue.

Now you want to select something for your dining-space

walls. "What do you recommend for my dinette?" you ask. "For dining rooms," says your informant, "everybody uses wallpaper." You didn't intend to get wallpaper. But you couldn't contradict an "expert," so you examine his samples. You stop to look at a rose-colored paper with a delicate, blue-green, vertical line. "I like the color, and the line will give height to the room," you think to yourself.

"You wouldn't want such a cheap kind," says the "expert." He turns to a blue-green, red and yellow floral pattern. "Now this is the finest paper we have," he announces. "It's hand-printed. We just sold thirty rolls to Mrs. Jones from the hill." The "expert" puts before your eyes *House and Palace* magazine. It carries an ad of the wallpaper. Yes, it must be a fine quality: the ad says so.

The double-barreled pressure from the "expert" and the magazine ad are too much to resist. You order the paper. You spend a sleepless night after making the purchase wondering whether you were right in accepting it. In a few days the paper is on the wall, and you and the multicolored floral design are to live with each other for a long time. You have other problems to think about, so you give no more thought to the wallpaper.

Now you are faced with the job of buying furniture. The living room is uppermost in your mind. You see an ad in the newspaper. The furniture looks good to you. The store's reputation is also good, and you decided to take a look at its wares. You are obviously a lady and look prosperous. "You want fine furniture, of course," says the salesman.

The furniture he shows you is the "latest." This is supposed to be synonymous with the most desirable. The salesman is not an "expert," for he is by classification a furniture salesman. The store has not given him any other title.

Hence he does not impose his opinion on you. There is no high pressure. He lets you look at other pieces. You come back to the first the salesman showed you.

You reveal that you like the style of the furniture: the simplicity appeals to you; the chairs look comfortable; the table has clean, smooth lines; the cabinets are neat looking. "We also have sofas and upholstered chairs in the same line," says the salesman, pointing out the pieces. "Why not furnish your entire home with this line? It's the best." Why not, you think. You find no objection.

Nevertheless, you would like to see this style of furniture in light-colored wood. But the light wood will not be in for about two months (which you know may mean four), and you want the furniture in two weeks. You order the furniture for the entire house from the same line that the salesman suggested.

The large upholstered pieces are covered in the most "fashionable" colors, chocolate brown with a metallic gold thread interwoven. Two side chairs are upholstered with the same material. The coffee table is covered with natural (brown) leather embossed in gold. "It's a nice accent," says the salesman. The rug department recommended brown carpeting. The drapery department provided another "accent." The draw draperies, the best available, are beige with a gold thread. A few Chinese pagoda lamps with gold square shades, some tables and pictures complete the living-room requirements.

Comes October 1; the decorating has been done. The living room wall is "forest green," the bedrooms are "chocolate brown." One bedroom was made a much lighter brown. "The room is too small for such a dark color," said the painter. Real reason: not having enough of the deep color left, he added white to increase the amount in order to have enough to finish the job. After the dinette was finished there was still some wallpaper left, and this was used on the west wall of the bathroom. The other walls were painted blue. The painter had too little blue for all four walls, because some of the blue paint accidentally landed in the wrong can.

The furniture and all living-room accessories arrive, as well as the furnishings for the other rooms. You give your best effort to the arrangement of the living room. You are not so particular about the other rooms; placing the dining-room and bedroom furniture is relatively simple. Now the home is complete. You are glad that the ordeal is over.

You alternate between satisfaction and disappointment. At the housewarming party, some of the visitors politely compliment you, and wish you the best in your new home. Others stare. They don't know what to say. "Looks like a nice expensive setup," remarks one friend. "I'm glad we got through all right," you say. But at the same time something seems vaguely amiss.

You have been in your new home about two weeks. Several times within this period your husband called to tell you that he had business engagements and couldn't come home to dinner. You become aware of feeling unusually out of sorts. "Maybe some knick-knacks for the house will give me a lift," you think. You ask yourself what you ought to shop for now.

18. Analysis of the Newly Furnished Home

Perhaps the person I just described is not you at all. It may be difficult for you to imagine this experience as yours. But it could be the experience of your neighbor or of thousands of other women. And whether or not you could

be persuaded to make the errors described above, you will
find it instructive to note the what and why of everything
that is wrong.

Let us analyze this interior which is so largely the result
of planless purchases and dubious salesmanship.

The sameness of the furniture pieces in the living room
produces an effect of monotony. Variety is lacking in the
height of the furniture pieces, in their proportions, in the
style of the legs. The wood is dark and stands against a
dark wall; the rug is brown and has even less contrast with
the furniture. The sofa is placed against the center of one
wall, and centered against the opposite wall is the fireplace
mantle.

Putting it another way, the neutral color tones are too
repetitious and too passive. The shapes of the furniture
pieces, all being identical in design, also produce the effect
of an excessively passive over-all pattern. The pictures,
which are all the same size, are hung in a line on each of
the two large opposite walls. This further increases the ultra-
passive, monotonous sensation. All the passive elements combined contribute to boredom. And the furniture against each
of the two large opposite walls, being perfectly symmetrical
in arrangement and thus static, also spells monotony.

The guests at the housewarming party undoubtedly felt
something of all this when they fell rather short of enthusiastic praise for the homemaker's efforts. In all probability,
however, they attributed their apathy to other causes than
the psychological effects of the surroundings.

Because the steady impressions of colors, images and
patterns affect us on an unconscious level, we tend to suppose that any dissatisfactions created by them must result
from factors impinging upon our consciousness. If wives and

husbands can't blame their malaise on each other or on their neighbors, they may blame it on the dog, the cat or the canary. They will hardly blame themselves; least of all, unless they are keenly aware of the psychological power of colors, shapes and arrangements, are they likely to blame an interior design.

The colors in a bathroom should be predominently warm, cozy, flattering to the skin. (Where else does your skin get the light, if not in your bathroom?) Here the blue walls produce the sensation of coldness instead of warmth. In this small space blue is reflected onto your skin and makes it look gray and unhealthy.

Even the bedrooms in this unhappy home do not achieve their purpose of promoting rest and pleasure. A bedroom has the advantage of being used most with the lights out, and color therefore does not play as great a part in it as in the living room or dining room. But chocolate brown walls in a bedroom do not bring contentment or inspiration.

Is it actually business engagements that prevent the husband from coming home to dinner? After all, he could invite his business guests to his home Quite possibly his unconscious aim is simply to escape eating in the newly decorated dining room. He may even believe that his wife's cooking has deteriorated, never dreaming of the effect of the surroundings on his appetite. If you remember the case described earlier in this book under the caption, "You Eat With Your Eyes," you will have no trouble understanding how negative visual sensations may cause digestive upsets.

An example of "sensation transference" is the case of a friend of mine who refused to have lunch in a certain restaurant "because the food is terrible." When the restaurant was modernized with an attractive and pleasant interior, I managed to induce him to try a luncheon in the newly decorated place. He declared the food excellent. "The decoration makes no difference to me," he said, "but the new cook is wonderful." Actually, the food was prepared by the same person, the owner of the restaurant.

Now let us return to our analysis of what is wrong with the home situation.

What about the wife? All day the black-green living-room walls subject her to an atmosphere of gloom. Her main escape is to the razzle-dazzle wallpaper in the dining room. Here the multicolored, aggressive, vibrant florals dance before her eyes, allowing her not a moment of peace as long as she is exposed to them. The home appears to offer a choice of dark monotony, chilling blue and neurotic over-stimulation, with perhaps a dash of glaring white in the kitchen. It is a discouraging outlook. It may even contribute to nervous indigestion.

You may be willing to concede some of these points but still find it hard to believe that poor room composition plus a bad color scheme can wreak quite so much havoc. "Ridiculous," you say. "An interior cannot possibly be that important. Why grandmother and grandfather lived with loud wallpaper all their lives, and it never caused any emotional problems."

You forget that grandfather had a much easier time of it in his office. Unlike your husband, he didn't strain his eyes day after day. He didn't undergo the tensions, the conflicts, the mounting pressures of modern life. On the contrary, he was probably bored most of the time. What appealed to him in a home was not so much an atmosphere of relaxation as a cluttered, gaudy environment, which he found stimulating rather than harassing because it was a welcome change from the whitewashed monotony in which he worked.

As for grandmother, she was probably a household drudge. She was always slaving in the kitchen or caring for the hundred-and-one pieces of bric-a-brac in the living room. She aged early and expected little from life. Existence was simple and tedious, and to compensate somewhat for her lack of varied, meaningful activity, she filled her living room with gingerbread and made her home into as busy-looking a place as possible.

Perhaps you have not fully realized that our industrial civilization has created new psychological needs. Though we still don't like to be bored or depressed, we come home primarily to relax. The wallpaper I have described does not provide a restful area for the eyes. It darts about, it causes blinking. It crowds the room. It advances. It menaces. It permits no tranquillity. It detracts from everything else. In short, it is an optical irritant and a psychological hazard. It is driving the occupants out of the house.

19. Your New Home After Color-Tuning

After you have read this book, you will know the difference between having furniture in matched pieces only and having varied but related pieces. You will know what it means to use related and complementary colors instead of monotonous or clashing ones. You will realize the importance of having lyrical and/or dramatic living space while avoiding both static arrangements and vibrating over-all pattern florals that are not conducive to pleasurable living. You will be aware that passive design should serve as the background for lyrical and/or dramatic arrangement of furniture.

You will learn how to judge self-styled "experts," and you will be able to make your own analysis of your needs in creating for yourself and for your family a living area that will promote emotional stability and general happiness.

For your living room, you will have furniture pieces in three or four matched sets, the style or design of which will be related in basic style. They will be in harmony because they will have a common denominator, that of design character. At the same time, each of the three or four sets will have distinct characteristics. For example, you will want a low coffee table, a tall game table, medium-height end tables, and the chairs will be of still another height. You will want a few pieces with round tops or round legs and some pieces with rectangular tops or rectangular legs. In other words, some of your furniture pieces will be related, some matched. Your interior will have variety, harmony and unity.

After reading this book carefully, you will not choose your wall color without analyzing at the same time the color of your furniture and rug. Nor will you choose a color simply because it is "fashionable" or because an "expert" says you should have it for no other reason than that Mrs. Jones bought it.

You will choose a color for the living-room walls as a background for your pictures. This will not be the same in tone or value as the large upholstered furniture pieces. You will have walls contrasting in value with that of the wood pieces, deep-toned walls for light wood, light-toned walls for dark wood.

You may use colors derived from the same hue for the walls and rug. Then you will have complementary colors in the upholstered pieces and drapery. If you prefer to have the walls complementary to the rug, then the upholstered pieces and draperies will be complementary to one or the other.

The dining room, dinette or dining space will be of

a color conducive to the enjoyment of food. The walls may be peach, raspberry or a soft green, never multicolored over-all floral patterns.

For your bedroom, you may decide on a luscious warm or exotic color with rich, vibrant accessories. Whether your bedroom furniture is rugged or dainty, conventional or modern, ornate or streamlined, you will not be indifferent to the colors.

In your bathroom, you will have tile or paint in a predominant pink, rose or other color of the red family that will reflect warmth. You may also have a grayed blue-green. And you will have a large mirror for the express purpose of helping you become more conscious of the beauty of your bodily proportions and skin color.

Your bathroom will assume its rightful importance in your life. From its former status as a minor adjunct of the home, it will become your headquarters for *l'art de toilette* and a place for pleasurable relaxation. It will add to your joy in life. Your friends will notice a happy change in you. The man in your life will compliment you on your new radiance. All this as the result of achieving a beautiful harmonious environment in your bathroom! Such is the power of color.

If you have a house instead of an apartment, you will wish to give attention to the color of the exterior. There, too, you will maintain a complementary and related color plan. With red brick, you will have a green trim or a tone of red. With yellow brick, you will choose a violet-blue tone or a muted yellow (beige). You will know that complementary combinations have greatest contrast and are most stimulating, while related tones are soft and less conspicuous.

Applying the foregoing principles in planning your home

furnishings will not solve any economic problem you may have. Having a living space that is harmonious and unified in color, form and arrangement will not cure any physical ills. However, providing an environment in which the colors are based on psychological-scientific principles will contribute vitally to your happiness and to the well-being of your entire family. All parts of your home will be correlated and coordinated, geared to creating an environment for happy living.

CHAPTER TWO

A Color Plan for Each Type of Room

1. Your Living Room

What colors to have in your living room depends on the following factors:

1. Your individual character, emotional make-up and background.
2. The nature of your family.
3. The availability of colors.
4. The colors you already have in some of your furnishings, such as a perfectly serviceable rug.
5. Your economic status, that is, whether you can throw out or sell for a song your unwanted color, in your rug for example, and get a new rug regardless of cost.
6. The kind of entertaining you do (after all, a living room

is the place where you receive guests; they, too, should be given consideration).

Is it the living room in which you and your family spend most of your time at home? If so, do you like a quiet, restful living room or do you prefer it gay and dramatic?

If you want the room to be restful, you are likely to prefer grayed blue walls, grayed green-blue walls or violet-gray walls; the rug should be in a neutral-complementary color. One pleasant, restful color scheme might include violet-gray walls with a gray-green rug. The upholstered furniture should be subdued, a delicate gray-green sofa, a couple of chairs in a predominantly deep violet-gray covering or one in deep green, with a few dark wood pieces such as a coffee table and end tables, as well as some pictures of the traditional school.

You may have a preference for grayed green-blue walls with a tan or beige rug, brown and tan upholstered furniture, light wood cocktail and end tables and a few smaller chairs in green-blue plus some calm, restful landscapes on the wall.

If you want the living room to be more festive in character, you may still have neutral green or violet-gray (gray with magenta red) walls and a light-toned complementary rug, but your upholstered furniture will then be in pure rich colors, perhaps magenta-red couches and neutral-green chairs with bleached mahogany or limed oak wood, colorful impressionist pictures and green draperies.

If you want an extremely dramatic room and are not afraid of light colors (because they show the slightest bit of soil), you may want a golden yellow sofa against a deep violet-blue background with a number of chairs covered in violet-blue, gold-colored draperies and a couple of large reproductions of Van Gogh paintings or originals by a contemporary artist whose work is dramatic.

As a considerate and loving wife, you will not want your living room to be dominated by a color for which your husband has an aversion. Of course, if you want to encourage him to go out evenings (or perhaps leave permanently), you can easily induce him to do so by liberally using a color for which he has a phobia. Color can be used either to invite or to repel. Once you discover that your man has a color phobia you can use the information for your own purposes.

To have a harmonious home you need not acquire exact shades, tints and tones. Fundamentally, all that is necessary is to have complementary and related colors. Whether the colors are a trifle lighter or darker than those shown on the color swatch makes little or no difference with regard to their visual or psychological aspects.

The important points to remember are that magenta reds go with greens, yellows with violet-blues, yellow-greens with violets, blue-greens with reds and green-blues with orange-reds.

Consult the color charts to find out what a color consists of. For example, you see a brown. Find out whether the brown is on an orange-red, red or magenta red chart. Or you want a gray-green. Is the gray-green based on yellow-green or blue-green, or is it made from yellow and gray (black plus white)? Consult the charts to get the right answers. The pure color is in the upper left-hand corner.

You should have no difficulty in obtaining the wall colors you want. Practically any color is available to you. Show the color charts in this book to the paint dealer. He will have the color ready-made, will mix it for you or will give you one or two basic colors and white with which to do your own mixing. Don't try to describe a color without having the color charts with you. Words are never specific enough to describe a color. Also have the color charts with you when you go shopping for draperies and other furnishings.

In upholstered furniture and draperies, you can't always get what you want at the price you can afford to pay. Since available colors in popular prices are limited, if you decide that you must have a color in one exact tone but cannot or will not pay the high cost of a special match, you are setting yourself an unreachable goal and inviting needless frustration. As noted above, a satisfactory scheme is not dependent on this or that specific tone, shade or tint.

Economic reasons also may prevent you from having a room perfectly balanced in furniture styling. For a number of years to come you may find it expedient to combine modern with traditional furniture. If your traditional pieces are simple in line and clean and smooth of surface, there will be no clash whatever between them and most contemporary styles.

Your present rug, if it is in a flat color related or complementary to the wall color, need not by any means be discarded. But if you have a multicolored, riotous pattern on the floor that draws your own gaze and that of everyone else to itself at the expense of guests and furnishings alike, I recommend that you save money on other things and get a new rug. My advice is the same for such a piece of furniture as an over-sized sofa with loud, gaudy florals that steal attention because of their dazzling, eye-irritating and psychologically overwhelming accents.

Important to your living room are color accents in the form of pictures and ceramics. In the objects that serve as accents you have an opportunity to incorporate the complementary colors in their pure state. Some small spots of another hue need not be kept out.

For example, if your room is furnished predominantly in browns, tans, green-blue tones and deep green-blues, you should have some brilliant orange ash trays or burnt orange ceramic figures and some pure turquoise pieces. These pure colors can be repeated in pictures, lamp shades, draperies.

Brilliant accents are very stimulating. They are effective eye-catchers and of interest to guests. If the objects providing the color accents have artistic merit—if they are original, creative pieces of sculpture and original paintings, they will be all the more significant.

With the information just given added to that in the discussion on page 47, there is no reason why you can't have a perfectly harmonious setting in your living room. It is certainly not difficult to get the right color of paint for the walls and to select draperies and furnishings of related and complementary colors. Striking accents, judiciously placed, will round out an attractive picture. The living room will measure up to its name!

2. The Master Bedroom

The bedroom is pre-eminently the place for relaxation, privacy and intimacy. In planning the colors and the furnishings in your living room you have to consider yourself, your family and your friends. In planning your bedroom, you have to consider only yourself and your man, if you happen to have one.

This is your chance to analyze your partner in life, his needs and peculiarities and at the same time to combine a little self-analysis with the project of planning the bed-room. First to be considered is whether or not your husband has any color phobias. Suppose his Aunt Tillie, who nearly always wore a mauve skirt, refused to let him have cookies and punished him severely whenever he was caught taking the sweets from the pantry. If that is the case, and if, as a result, your husband has acquired a strong dislike for mauve, you should under no circumstances have mauve walls or draperies in the bedroom (or any other room). Neither should you wear anything mauve if you cherish your hus-band's love.

Leaving out colors for which either your spouse or you have an aversion, you are free to choose any hue as the basis for your dominant color. Your attitude toward bedrooms will determine not only the basic hue but also the tone of the color. You may consider the bedroom primarily a place for relaxation; if so, you will choose a delicate, neutral blue-green or green-blue.

But you may be one of those who relax only with eyes shut. Obviously, color is not then a factor in your relaxa-tion. Instead of a relaxing color, you may want a vibrant one that will inspire you to get out of bed as soon as there is light and you are awake. Similarly, you may want a color that will aid your husband to rise in the morning.

For this purpose, rose or a rich pink, composed of white and red, is a wonderful color for bedroom walls. It is exotic and vibrant. It leads to action and is not at all conducive to leisurely meditation or open-eyed daydreaming. This may be just the incentive you and your mate need to "get going," where a delicate blue wall would be likely to encourage wakeful lingering in bed because it is cool, soothing and associated with the restful open sky.

Green bedroom walls are an advantage in an industrial community. If you can't have trees in front of your window, you can put green paint on the walls, with magenta-red draperies providing the stimulating complement. It is amazing what a potent substitute green paint is for foliage.

Perhaps the ideal bedroom is one with pink walls and green draperies, looking out upon evergreens in front of the windows. In temperate climates, evergreens, such as white pine, arborvitae or spruce, provide green for pleasant sensation all year round.

If there is not much natural sunlight in your bedroom, yellow walls are advisable. Violet or violet-blue draperies will make the yellow more vibrant. With yellow, however, you must use caution. If the yellow is too strong it may cause headaches.

Then too, many people have a strong dislike for yellow. Tests conducted by Color Research Institute show that fewer than 10 per cent have an aversion to red, green or blue, while more than 40 per cent have an aversion to yellow.

Should the bedroom-wall colors be deep or light? The answer to this question depends on the amount of natural light in the room, on the type of furniture and on the size of the room.

If the light is poor, it would be a mistake to have deep-toned walls. Dark colors "eat up" light. The surfaces in a room are just as much a factor in illuminating the interior as is the light source. If the natural light in the room is very strong, deep-toned walls are beneficial because they absorb much of the excess light and have a minimum of glare. Generally, middle tones are ideal, because they provide neither excessive nor insufficient contrast for dark and light furnishings.

If your furniture wood is dark, you should under no circumstances have deep-toned walls. Lack of contrast between furniture and wall is unpleasant. Dark against dark is monotonous, hard on the eyes and psychologically negative. If you have light wood bedroom pieces and illumination is not a factor, deep-toned walls are appropriate because the light-colored furniture stands out against the dark background.

Important to keep in mind is that deep and warm colors will make your bedroom look smaller, whereas light colors will make the interior appear more spacious. If a room seems crowded, deep colors on the walls will add to the cramped appearance.

You will find it worthwhile to study lighting as an important factor in color effect. You should be aware that illumination is an element in being seen as well as in seeing. The same kind of lighting is not equally good for both. Although white fluorescent light is best for seeing, it is not an ideal light in which to be seen. Better is the yellowish incandescent light bulb. A magenta-red or rose light is most flattering to the skin. It is soft. It glows. It provides ideal illumination for the bedroom, if the main objective is to be seen under the most favorable conditions and if the lighting is not meant for a seeing activity such as for reading in bed.

If you wish to have illumination to accomplish both objectives—to show yourself in the best light and also to provide proper lighting for reading in bed—you should have your bedroom equipped with two lamps, the shade for one lamp being white or opaque and for the other a translucent pink, rose or magenta-red. The colored lamp should be on only when the white one is out.

With white illumination, indirect lighting is much more flattering than light that strikes directly from the lamp.

Light that is reflected from the ceiling is diffused and soft and tends to wash away wrinkles. Interesting and striking shadows may be produced by lighting from one side.

Bedroom furniture should be chosen primarily for its physical function. Drawer space is, of course, an important element to consider. If you are buying new furniture for your bedroom and you aren't a slave to tradition, you are likely to be happiest with pieces that are basically functional, simple in line and soft and neutral in color. Wood that is natural in color, neither stained nor bleached, is easiest on the eyes and is pleasing against deep-toned walls as well as against very light-tinted walls.

Draperies should be complementary to the color of the walls so that they may serve as a frame for the window and at the same time provide an effect of both variety and harmony. For pink or rose walls, you should have green draperies, for green walls, rose (or magenta-red) draperies. For peach (orange-red plus white) walls, green-blue draperies are needed, and for green-blue walls, peach or burnt orange window panels. For yellow walls you need violet-blue draperies, and for violet-blue walls, yellow draperies. Of course, the drapery colors need not be flat; they may have a pattern. But the dominant color should be complementary to the walls.

Pictures for the bedroom walls should also be chosen on the basis of an analysis of your husband's and your own personalities. First of all, I want to point out that the wall facing you when you are in bed should have no pictures. You don't want anything on the wall to attract or hold your attention when you are in bed.

Except for the wall facing you, you should use as many pictures as there is wall space for hanging them. The kind of pictures to choose also should be part of your spouse-and-self analysis. If neither of you is neurotically inhibited, if you are both in the habit of expressing yourselves naturally and if you do not feel Puritanically repressed in the bedroom, you may find it suitable to have pictures that illustrate or symbolize love on your bedroom walls.

Portraits are not appropriate for a bedroom because, as was already pointed out, the bedroom is for you and your husband. No other personality, dead or alive, should be in your *chambre à coucher*. Portraits are personalities. They can contribute to the interest and activity of the living room, but their eyes should not be permitted to intrude upon the privacy of the bedroom.

Abstract paintings, in my opinion, do not belong in the bedroom. Geometric patterns are often quite intriguing and arresting. But such forms and patterns are rather incongruous in your intimate quarters. In the living room, over the fireplace, yes, if you enjoy abstract art, but it does not give the kind of effect that you welcome in the bedroom, which is a place for warmer and more concrete appreciations than those afforded by the austere beauty of geometric lines.

Nor do landscapes generally enrich a bedroom, though they may be permissible if they show romantic scenes, colorful and emotion-rousing. However, if you and your husband (not *or* your husband) are the outdoor type, you may enjoy having a lively, realistic and rugged landscape in your bedroom.

The ideal form of pictorial art for a bedroom is probably the nude. The nude in a bedroom is in its natural environment. The nude is impersonal. It does not scrutinize you from the wall. You look up at it instead. If possible, the picture should be in natural colors. However, the undraped female figure is attractive even in black and white.

I sincerely urge every homemaker, every potential promoter of a happy home, to get at least one work of art of a nude figure or preferably two impersonal female nudes for the bedroom. Don't ask your husband to buy these pictures —you get them.

If pictures of beautiful nudes are in your bedroom, their pervasive loveliness is bound to work its charm. They will widen the area of sensations and experiences shared both consciously and unconsciously by you and your husband. They may add remarkably to your mutual contentment with life.

Never underestimate the importance of a bedroom. It is a question whether the living room or the bedroom is the most important room in the house. A color-tuned living room will be filled with guests as often as you invite them. A color-tuned bedroom will help you to retire, will inspire you in making a vigorous start in the morning. But what is paramount, a carefully planned bedroom, as outlined here, can make an important contribution to marital happiness.

3. The Dining Area

Dining rooms are fast disappearing, but dining will always stay with us whether the space in which we eat is part of the living room or of the kitchen. Earlier in this book, I gave you some indication of the effect of colored lights on food and the consequent impact on the appetite. Now let me tell you more of what we have found out about color in relation to dining.

You may not know, or perhaps I should say it's unusual if you are fully aware, that ordinary colors have an effect on your appetite. We have all kinds of evidence demonstrating that color plays a great part in the enjoyment of food. Food experts know that the appetite is conditioned by the sense of sight just as much as by the sense of smell. This is well illustrated by the reluctance of most people to eat margarine of a cold, white appearance but their enjoyment of it when it is colored a warm, soft yellow.

Colors affect eating in two ways, as part of the food and as elements of the surroundings in which you eat. Experiments and studies have indicated that those colors in the food itself which have appetite-appeal also contribute to hearty appetite if they are part of the surroundings. Peach, raspberry, warm greens, light and deep browns usually stimulate the appetite. These are, therefore, ideal colors for your dining room or dining space.

An outstanding example of the importance of surface colors in connection with eating was the experience of the owner of a well-known chain of eating places. Originally his idea was to create an atmosphere of cleanliness by having pure white walls of shining tile. Business, however, was not good.

The restaurant-operator then introduced color into a few of his places. These did so much more business than the white-tiled establishments that he soon changed the interiors in all of them. This case strongly suggests that large white spaces are psychologically negative and uninviting, at least as far as food consumption is concerned.

Which particular colors to choose often depends on other than objective appetite factors. There are further psychological considerations. Perhaps your husband or one of your offspring has a phobia in relation to raspberry, entirely conscious and due to some deeply felt experience associated with the color in the past.

What can be even worse is an aversion to a color without any awareness of it, or without acknowledgment by the person involved because he believes his reaction to be silly. Rationally he may condemn his dislike as nonsense; but our emotions are not rational. If a person has a phobia about raspberry, he may not be able to enjoy the food at a table that is surrounded by raspberry walls.

I knew a man who had an allergy to raspberries, breaking out with a rash after eating them. Raspberry color made him feel ill and caused complete loss of appetite, although there was no evidence that a raspberry color on the wall gave him a rash.

A young lady of my acquaintance refused to eat in a room with green walls or green upholstered furniture. This color phobia was traced to an early childhood experience in which she became very ill from drinking a liquid that was green in color. She had attributed her illness to the drink but was not aware that her aversion to green was associated with that experience until it was traced and pointed out to her.

What was most unusual about this case was that the young lady had no objection to green anywhere except in a place where food was served. At a picnic she had a wonderful time playing ball on the grass and listening to her boy friend strumming his ukulele. But when eating time came she insisted on going into the pavilion. If such a young lady were your daughter, you, of course, would not have green walls in your dining room.

The type of illumination in your dining room will have a great effect on the appetite. I consider it particularly important to discuss this aspect because in recent years the trend has been to install cold fluorescent lighting in homes. Most fluorescent tubes provide an entirely different kind of light from that of incandescent bulbs.

The following case illustrates the effect of wrong lighting on food. A business executive took a guest to a restaurant in which the host regularly dined. The proprietor was very proud of the special lighting he had just installed. Being in high spirits and wanting to help his old customer make a good impression on his guest, the proprietor asked the chef to prepare an especially fine, rich, brown chicken. But when the chicken was served it was a sickly, unappetizing gray. Three times the chicken was returned to the kitchen; three times it came back, looking sicklier with each trip. When the new lights were removed and the old type of lighting re-installed, food ceased changing color on the way from the kitchen to the dining room.

Remember that surface colors are greatly affected by the type of illumination. When you are planning color for a dining room you must include the lighting in your plan as well as the surface colors. The common incandescent electric bulb provides a warm, yellowish light. There are three types of fluorescent light: blue, daylight and yellow. The last is the closest in character to the incandescent bulb type of light. Cold and warm fluorescent types of light can be used effectively for different and special purposes.

Where the intention is to encourage people to be leisurely, yellow or warm lighting is very effective because it flatters the complexion, creates a sense of coziness, produces the effect of warmth and induces the desire to relax.

A blue fluorescent light is unflattering. Cold light is not romantic. It is sharp and glaring.

In a quick-service sandwich shop, cold daylight may be ideal for business because it encourages people to eat quickly and get out. This is not what you want for the room where you entertain your guests.

Psychologically, the cold light inspires the idea (enter-tained consciously or unconsciously) that you may as well be outside; it seems no different indoors. This is particularly true in the summertime when fresh air is an additional incentive to go out. But the enticements of the outdoors are hardly strong enough to overcome the lure of a pleasant evening meal enjoyed in the midst of soft, warm lights, attractive surface colors and congenial company.

In the dining room, complementary colors play an important part physically, visually and thus psychologically. The optical phenomenon of the after-image, discussed in the first chapter, can be used in the dining room to make an important contribution to appetite appeal.

A colored dish that complements the color of the food saturates the eye with the color, causing an after-image that enhances the appearance of the food. For example, a blue-green plate makes cooked meat look browner and richer. A deep red plate makes a salad look greener and fresher.

However, in planning color you must think of the effect of the entire table setting. A table with dishes of various colors does not produce an orderly, coordinated effect. It lacks unity.

The way to make maximum use of complementary colors in planning a table setting is to establish a color relationship between the color plan of the room and the dishes, tablecloth, napkins and centerpiece.

For example, if your dining area is color-tuned with peach and a green-blue tone, you might use peach and grayed green-blue dishes with a white or neutral color tablecloth. You could use peach dishes on a tablecloth of a tint or tone of green-blue or white dishes on a tablecloth of a deep green-blue shade. There are many ways in which you can vary the desired effect from day to day or from meal to meal by thoughtful planning and selection of your table accessories to delight your family and friends.

One hostess, who is noted for her buffet dinners, uses a deep red (raspberry) tablecloth, red or green napkins and deep green dishes. As a rule she has a bowl of red roses in the center of the table and she always serves two large molded gelatin salads, one red, the other green, with garnishes that heighten the red-green effect. The over-all effect is very appealing.

The guests are lavish in their praise of the "wonderful food." Although the food she serves is always well prepared, I have reason to believe that much of the guests' enthusiasm and acclamation is a case of "sensation transference." The guests transfer the pleasing sensation from the table-setting to the food.

Obviously, the colors in an eating situation are just as important as the taste and the odor. People "eat with their eyes." A scientifically planned color scheme, appropriate furnishings and the right lighting in your dining room can make an important contribution to the enjoyment of your food.

4. Your Kitchen

Not too many years ago the kitchen was a cluttered, ugly place in which, however, some very tasty food was often prepared. To the homemaker of the nineteenth century, beauty was associated with the living room, not with the kitchen. Aesthetics belonged in the front parlor or drawing room and seldom, if ever, found its way into the kitchen.

Grandmother's stove was far from being a thing of beauty, and the icebox was, as the name suggests, just that—a mere box. The walls were generally whitewashed, and if grandfather was a good provider, there were copper cooking utensils hanging on the lower part of at least one of the walls.

Usually a cast-iron skillet and a pot or two were perched on the top of the stove.

The modern kitchen has nothing in common with grandmother's except that it, too, is used for preparing food. In many contemporary homes, of all the rooms, the kitchen is the most beautiful; it has lost all resemblance to the kitchen of the last century. Equal modernization cannot be attributed to contemporary living rooms filled with imitations of sixteenth, seventeenth and eighteenth century furniture. It may be that you spend more time in the kitchen than you do in the living room and therefore are of the opinion that the color and design in the kitchen are more important to you.

Kitchen-equipment design has the advantage of not being hampered by tradition. The designer of an electric stove can't follow traditional concepts of design because there are no traditional electric stoves. The designer is free to create kitchen equipment by considering only physical function and "eye appeal." Therefore the forms and lines in the modern kitchen are smooth, lyrical, rarely obtrusive. There is nothing you can do or are likely to want to do about changing the design of your recently acquired refrigerator or dishwasher because it is already streamlined, easy to use and easy to look at.

You can, however, make a great contribution to the psychological benefits of your kitchen by introducing appropriate colors. The walls and floors are important in the kitchen, and that is where you are free to provide suitable effects without interfering with the physical functions of the food-preparing and food-preserving appliances.

There is no doubt that the streamlined stove is much more pleasant to look at than the old-fashioned model adorned with cast-iron floral designs. (The ornamentation was intended to compensate for the ugliness of the form.) The modern refrigerator, sink and kitchen cabinets are easy on the eyes as images but in color are far from having an equally happy effect. The white and chromium reflect too much light and leave a psychologically negative impression.

For visual comfort and psychological benefit, the kitchen should have as many areas as possible that are easy on the eyes and psychologically pleasing. Therefore, all clear wall space should be treated with appropriate color of tile or paint.

The choice of hue depends primarily on your own personality. If you want a color stimulant in the kitchen, you will put a vibrant peach (a mixture of orange-red and white) on the walls and have a few warm red pieces of pottery on a shelf, in addition to some in complementary green-blue.

If you are of a nervous temperament, however, you will do best to have green walls in your kitchen with a few wine-red or raspberry red ceramic pieces as accents.

If you get no direct sunlight in your kitchen, it is advisable, unless you have an aversion to yellow, to introduce yellow walls that will suggest a feeling of sunshine. In this case you will appreciate some violet-blue spots in the form of pottery or water pitchers.

Too much direct sunlight may indicate the need of a delicate tone of blue wall to counteract the excessive yellow light. The blue wall will look richer and pleasanter if you have a few yellow ceramics about, where they will catch your attention or impress your unconscious from time to time.

Whichever hue you choose, the color on the wall should be neither very light nor very dark. If it is too light, it will not have sufficient contrast with the white kitchen equipment. If the color is very dark the contrast will be too great, and the strain on the eyes will be even worse than the monotony of having not enough contrast.

The ideal floor covering is one that has complementary colors, one color like that of the walls, the other similar to the accents (pottery or pitcher). The colors on the floor may or may not be of the same tone as the walls or the accents. For example, if the walls are green, the green on the floor may be either exactly the same in tone, more brilliant, lighter or darker. The red on the floor, however, while it may be lighter or darker than the accent pieces, should not be more brilliant or more pure in hue.

A vibrant color on a large floor area would distract you too greatly from your work in the kitchen. If the brilliant vibrant color is within your line of vision, no matter which way you turn your eyes, it will be a definite strain on your nervous system. In a working place, vibrant colors should occur only in small spots or objects to break the monotony, but never flood the eyes at every turn.

If a kitchen floor-covering is not available in colors that complement one another you can choose one flat or broken color. The color may be either related to or the complement of the color of the walls. Should you decide on a related color, you may have a deeper or lighter tone and are free to match the walls if you can and want to do so. For green walls, however, a magenta red, wine or raspberry red will be more dramatic and stimulating without being too vibrant and distracting.

You can generally get complementary colors in linoleum tile and other flooring material. You should not try to combine the colors without the aid of the color charts. If two colors are on facing charts, you know they are complementary. Your selections need not be exact matches in tone to the colors on the charts, but they should be close.

The working counter is as important in your kitchen as an inspection table in the industrial plant. The hue of the working counter may be the same as that of the walls or that of the floor. However, the color should be of a *middle* value, providing neither too little nor too much contrast for food preparation.

For greatest eye-ease, a work surface should reflect from 40 to 60 per cent of light. If you cannot have the same color as that of the walls or that of the floor, it is best to have a neutral color, gray or a natural wood color, warm yet sufficiently neutral. A plastic material should be used to provide a hard, heat- and stain-resistant working surface. Plastic surfacing materials, sold under various brand names, are available in a great choice of colors, including natural wood color.

If you dine in your kitchen, it is necessary to consider the color elements suitable for a dining room as well as for a kitchen.

5. The Nursery

"Baby" pink and "baby" blue are as factual as statements that "the sun sets" and "the sun rises." The sun doesn't set or rise, and your baby does not see pink or light blue. An infant cannot identify these colors if he is much less than a year old.

Most women like the tints derived from red and blue. Baby, however, enjoys the colors in their pure state, colors like vibrant red and brilliant blue. Red is normally the favorite with older children as well as with infants.

We have seen how a baby will prefer a red toy to a blue one. Apparently the love for red is instinctive. Young children love red; older children love it; teen-agers love it; most adults love it. But adults won't always admit that they do. Grown-ups are often inhibited. Many adults consider the warm red too loud, in bad taste (at least they say so). Unconsciously, most people feel attracted toward red; they enjoy it, but they also appreciate the intriguing qualities of lights and shadows, and they have learned to take the warm red color and all other stimulants in moderation. Children do not believe in moderation, and infants do not know what moderation is.

When it comes to your baby's room you are interested in two things—the baby's health and his happiness. For his health you want an airy, light room, for his happiness a lot of toys in red and in as many other bright colors as you can get. Free space to roam in, ample nourishment, fresh air, sunshine and plenty of bright-colored toys are baby's idea of heaven.

Experiments with children of different ages indicate that reds and greens are the ideal colors for infants' rooms. Magenta red and green do very well in the playroom. Orange-red and green-blue as well as red and blue-green make a good showing in both the nursery and the kindergarten. These colors remain the most effective for several years.

Blue-green walls and red miniature furniture are excellent. The blue-green should be a little grayed so that it will keep the red from vibrating and also not show your darling's finger marks too clearly.

A green cotton rug (which can be laundered often) is advisable. The red toys are easily seen on a green rug, whether the tone of the green is light or dark.

Should you use yellow and violet-blue for your baby's room if you happen to like this combination of colors? The answer is a definite "no." Color-preference tests conducted with children demonstrated that combinations of yellow and violet-blue and of yellow-green and violet are not the choice of most boys and girls. Nor did infants take to objects in these colors. When the blues and yellows won preference, there was usually some question about the child's emotional normality.

Yellow and violet-blue are for people who have absorbed life's lights and shadows. These are colors and qualities that require mature personalities, since violet-blue may be considered the shadow of yellow, a symbol of sunlight. They . are often exotic attractions for the sophisticated. For infants and children of all ages, however, they are sterile.

A young child's art shows only line and color—mostly reds and greens. Yellow does not vibrate enough—it is too weak and sickly for an active child; violet-blue is too dark, too deep. It has the fullest value through its conscious or unconscious symbolism, which is meaningless to a child.

If you want dramatic and exotic surroundings for yourself, you may choose violet-blue and yellow or violet and yellow-green (chartreuse).

Baby pink and baby blue you should reserve for your own room, for they may give you much pleasure if you love subtle, soft, delicate vibrations of visible energy. For your baby's room, red and green are the right colors.

6. The Study

Obviously, when we realize the psychological factors in color we recognize that a school boy's or girl's study should be given a color treatment different from that of other rooms. It should now be apparent that each room should be treated in relation to the character of its occupants, to the activities carried on in the room, to the room's dimensions and to its light source. Rooms for children should be planned to meet their psychological needs, not to please the parents' personal taste.

In the past "study" and "school" meant physical and mental drudgery in a poorly lighted and stuffy room. Modern study rooms and schoolrooms, however, are intended to provide for our children favorable lighting conditions and a healthful environment. Educational leaders now recognize that physical surroundings are vital psychological factors in study situations.

Educators are very much aware of the fact that education for modern living requires the integration and correlation of many elements. Courses are planned in relation to each other, and mental and physical studies are coordinated for the purpose of developing the children into well-integrated adults. Modern progressive education is geared to the demands of modern living.

Excellent physical facilities are now provided by all progressive school systems. Environment and atmosphere conducive to study and learning are considered essential. Comfortable desks and proper lighting are recognized as basic needs in all schoolrooms. Educators have encouraged furniture designers to develop posture chairs. Modern schoolroom seats no longer are cluttered with functionless design and disturbing ornamentation.

Educational authorities are cooperating with lighting engineers in developing more efficient lighting for the schoolroom. But not much study has been given to color, and the fact that color and light are interdependent is being widely disregarded.

Appropriate colors are important factors in providing

visibility as an aid to study, as well as in creating an environment that is conducive to study and which promotes physical and mental health. Study at home has the same requirements as study at school.

We should be aware that surfaces are just as important in efficient lighting as are the lighting fixtures and bulbs. We should remember that lighting includes a light source and a reflecting surface. The light source may be sunlight, an incandescent light bulb or a fluorescent tube. The lighting may be either direct from the light source or indirect, in which case the light is focused toward the ceiling so that reflected light illuminates the room. Whatever the type of lighting, the colors on the ceiling and walls are important factors in illumination of a room intended for study.

For the ceiling, white is desirable because it reflects maximum light. It cannot be psychologically negative because the student doesn't look at the ceiling, or at least shouldn't. For walls, white is most undesirable. Here the right use of color is important. If the correct wall color is not used, the walls will be either too dark and absorb too much light, or they will be too light and create blinding glare.

Continuous reading or writing tires the eyes, and it is necessary at certain intervals for the reader to turn away from the paper or book. To shift the gaze from a white paper to a white or near-white wall provides no relief. However, turning from a white sheet to a dark surface is anything but restful. On the contrary, shifting back and forth between very light and very dark surfaces means that the eyes have to make extreme adjustments which, if repeated often, are injurious. Only a medium tone can provide eye comfort after a period of concentration on reading or writing.

Just as important as the lighting from reflection is the psychological aspect of the color. Too many study rooms are depressing places. Nervousness, irritability and lack of interest in learning can often be traced to improper color in the study or room where studying is done.

We should remember that the light reflection factor is determined by the value of the color (lightness or darkness). The psychological effect is produced by the hue (red, blue, yellow and so on) as well as by the value of the color.

Warm, bright colors should not be used for the large areas in a study. It is advisable to have a blue or green-blue tone for the walls if other factors do not forbid it. For example, you would certainly find blue unsuitable, both if the occupant had an aversion to the color or if the room received natural light only from the north. Green is generally a safe color because it is rarely too cold or too warm.

An orderly environment inspires orderliness. Chaotic surroundings breed chaotic thinking and irrational behavior. The design of the furniture pieces and their arrangement are as important as the right color combinations in creating a favorable environment for study.

Furniture that is simple in form, smooth in finish and clean in line is most conducive to concentration. Furniture that is ornate, carved or cluttered with superimposed pattern is distracting.

A pleasing room arrangement is so proportioned that it has variety and harmony. In other words, the relationship of the various objects to one another should be such that they will have a common character or appear to belong to the same family, even though they may be varied in color-tone, shape and dimensions.

A room that has simply-designed furniture proportionately arranged, with colors on the walls of the right hue and tone, creates an atmosphere favorable to concentration and clear thinking.

7. The Playroom

"I invested a lot of money in fixing up a playroom in the basement, but the children won't use it," said my host. "They go to the neighbor's playroom, which is not nearly so well equipped. I don't understand why."

After seeing both my host's basement and the neighbor's, I understood why very well. My host's play space was orderly. It was whitewashed with the idea of giving the room "a clean look." It had the clean look of a nineteenth-century hospital room or a temporary emergency station.

The white walls were bleak and uninspiring. He had not realized that white has no appeal to children. Children have few or no color preferences based on associations. The white has not the same symbolism of purity, virginity and cleanliness for children that it has for their parents. White is unstimulating. It reflects nearly all of the light. The glare is an irritant and discourages play. In short, white is the wrong color for the walls of a playroom.

The neighbor's playroom was no larger. It is possible that the difference in cost was due to the fact that my host had an expensive-looking aluminum game table, whereas the neighbor had an ordinary wooden one.

But the neighbor's walls were burnt orange (a tone of orange-red), and the center part of the ceiling was painted a clear green-blue which gave the impression that it was much higher than it really was. A three-foot border of ceiling at the walls was painted white with indirect light fixtures distributed every six feet. The reflected light circled the room around the green-blue ceiling center.

The colors and lighting were dramatic and stimulating. The reflected light did not strike directly at the eyes as it would have done from a white wall, and the colors were "play colors."

The orange-red tone of the walls was rich and vibrant, and the light green-blue ceiling cool and soothing. Both colors produced an effect of the outdoors. The color scheme was optically and psychologically balanced. The lighting was easy on the eyes. The surroundings were inviting and inspired activity.

The children enjoyed spending their time in this color-tuned playroom. Adults felt comfortable in it. Yet it was not costliness that was the basis for its success. Planning of color and light made it what it was, a pleasure to be in for both young and old.

My host's lack of awareness of the importance of color and his ignorance about its optical and psychological characteristics were responsible for his children's discontent and for the habit they had formed of going away from home.

Failure to apply scientific color principles in the playroom may be the seed from which can grow estrangement between parents and children and even, as an end result, delinquency.

Remember that the right colors cost little or no more than wrong ones. Keep in mind that colors are major factors in illumination and have a significant bearing on sight. What is most important is that the colors in the surroundings are a psychological power for good or for bad because they bring about basic sensations which influence emotions and are involved in the building of behavior patterns.

If you value your children's happiness, if you want your children to grow up emotionally stable and in good health, you will not minimize the importance of having the right surroundings for your children when they are at play. By right surroundings, I mean particularly a room in which the colors and lighting are planned so that the place is easy on the eyes, inviting, conducive to healthful activity and contributive to emotional stability.

8. The Home Workshop

If your husband has a workshop where he practices his hobby, you will probably want to share this chapter, if not the entire book, with him. You will certainly want to show it to him for the help it can give him in preserving his eyesight, enjoying his hobby to the utmost and contributing to the greatest possible emotional stability—help in the form of planning optimum work-conditions of good lighting and proper color surroundings.

Seeing incorporates at least four elements—eyesight, light, contrast and the size and shape of object.

Good vision, achieved if necessary with the aid of glasses, is essential in all work situations where critical seeing is called for.

Different types of work call for varying amounts of illumination. For work requiring precision, such as detailed mechanical drawing, from 50 to 100 foot-candles of light are generally used. For most art work or for sawing, from 25 to 50 foot-candles are recommended. For general shop work, from 10 to 20 foot-candles are required. (In your laundry, from 5 to 10 foot-candles are sufficient.) Lighting is sometimes inefficient, not because there is not enough of it but because there is too much.

Working with contrasting colors does not require as much light as working with colors lacking contrast. For example, you need much more light for sewing brown cloth with brown thread than for sewing brown cloth with white or light green thread. Inefficient lighting and improper contrast contribute greatly to wastage of time and materials.

It is commonly recognized that it is more difficult to see a small object than a large one. It is also evident that the finer the work, the more illumination is required.

In the workshop, as in other rooms, lighting comes not only directly from the light source—daylight, incandescent bulb or fluorescent tube—but is also reflected from the surfaces in the interior—ceiling, walls, worktables and other objects.

Direct or reflected glare and harsh contrast of light or shade are the greatest enemies of good vision. Direct glare is usually caused by unshaded light, by shades that do not fully cover the bulbs and by lights that are too close to the line of vision. Reflected glare is caused by glossy or polished surfaces, white or near-white backgrounds and poor location of light sources.

When a person works or reads in a dark room under a spotlight or views television in a totally dark room his eyes are injured. The contrast between the strong light and the surrounding darkness causes eye fatigue which, if continued for a long period of time, injures the eyes.

Diffused light is the best kind of illumination for work, reading or any other kind of close application. Diffusion of light can be accomplished by having the light go through an opal glass fixture or by directing the light rays toward the ceiling to obtain indirect illumination by reflection.

Where there are surfaces and light there is color, and

where there is color there is psychological effect. When the objective is to secure a favorable psychological effect, you should know that it can be achieved with appropriate, scientifically chosen colors.

The color of the ceiling is a vital factor in illumination. If the ceiling is not within the line of vision, the psychological power of color need not be considered. In such instances, a white paint should by all means be applied to the ceiling to allow maximum light reflection. However, if the ceiling is within the line of vision, as is often true in a large space, a delicate tint will have a favorable psychological effect and cause only a slight loss in light reflection.

For the average work situation, colors that reflect from 40 to 60 per cent of the light are generally appropriate for walls. The neutral walls will provide sufficient contrast for both light and dark objects.

You should always remember that walls are more than physical barriers. Their function is not limited to keeping out rain and cold or enclosing and protecting property. Walls are also psychological factors and in addition serve a purpose in illumination.

The floor, like the ceiling and walls, should be considered from the psychological as well as from the lighting aspect. A dirty-looking, gray-black floor exerts a strong negative psychological effect and absorbs a good deal of light which instead should be used to advantage.

In many types of work good visibility is essential from below, no less than from above. A light tone can be put on the floor to provide the needed brightness for reflecting light and, at the same time, to contribute great psychological value.

Worktables present both psychological and visibility problems. The working surface of the table can easily become a means for increasing efficiency, merely by being treated with a color that neither absorbs nor reflects too much light.

In short, use of appropriate colors properly in a workroom will provide correct visibility and favorable psychological environment, both of which result in greater efficiency and accomplishment.

office   The following are the major factors which you should keep in mind when planning your workroom or utility room:

1. Cheerful surroundings make you cheerful. Drab colors make you sluggish.
2. A warm place of work can be made to look cooler by having surroundings in cool colors.
3. A cool place of work can be made to look warmer by having surroundings in warm colors.
4. Deep colors on walls and furniture absorb much light, require more foot-candles of light and result in large electric bills.
5. Light colors reflect most of the light and aid in illuminating the interior, thus providing proper light at less cost.
6. Work backgrounds (walls, tables) that are too light or too dark cause eye fatigue and cut down efficiency.
7. Glossy surfaces cause eye fatigue and hinder work.
8. Mat or dull surfaces and surfaces that have proper contrast to the material you work on will aid you in your work.

9. The Guest Room

The guest room should be looked upon as a combination living room and bedroom. You shouldn't be subjective in choosing the colors for this room. Your own favorite color combination may not be pleasing to most people.

Possibly you have a fetish for a certain color. Your abnormally strong love for this color may be due, let's say, to an unconscious association of this color with a childhood love for an attractive teacher in grammar school, who had a number of garments of that color. Of course, you are not aware that your attraction to the color is based on this juvenile infatuation. As far as you are concerned, you like the color, and that is all.

To your guests the color may be a strong irritant. A sure way to discourage week-end guests is to choose a dominant color with a low percentage of general preference. If you appreciate guests you will choose a dominant color that has a very high preference rating, that is, a color that appeals to the greatest number, whether or not it happens to be your favorite.

Tones derived from blue-green and green-blue are safe for the walls of a guest room because they have popular appeal. More than 90 per cent of all people enjoy looking at tones derived from these two hues. That is why we say that they are colors with high preference ratings.

If you happen to have a dislike for blue-green and green-blue, disregard your attitude toward the colors in this case. You should eliminate your own emotional reactions when planning a guest room. Your friends should be given primary consideration here—that is unless you are completely self-centered and indifferent toward them.

A common error is to choose a "fashionable" color for the guest room. You will not do this if you are aware that a color may be "in fashion" without having a high preference rating. "Fashion" is not always, in truth rarely, based on scientific data. And, as I have already quoted, "Those who follow fashion blindly have no taste."

The fact that a color is advocated by a paint company

or is advertised in a magazine does not mean that it is necessarily a color that has wide appeal. It may merely mean that
the manufacturer or the advertiser hopes to promote greater
acceptance of the color by constant repetition of its true or
imaginary merits.

One well-meaning housewife "redecorated" her guest
room, together with most of the rest of the house, in chartreuse and olive green because a magazine advocated the
use of these two colors. Both she and her husband were
much pleased with the new color scheme. Her home was
isolated, away from public transportation, difficult for
friends to visit. But she had always enjoyed week-end guests.
Her husband had a high income, and she could afford an
expensively furnished home, the attractions of which had
overcome its relative inaccessibility.

During the four years since they had bought the house,
guests came nearly every week end. But during the five
months following their "redecoration," they had only two
week-end guests. Most visitors decided to go home early
in the evening. Even when leaving meant braving a winter
storm, the guests insisted that they could not remain.

I was one of two guests who accepted an invitation to stay
overnight.

In the guest room, the chartreuse hit me between the eyes
as soon as I entered the doorway. The olive green lamp
shades, olive green bedcover and olive green draperies were
areas to which I immediately directed my gaze to escape the
sickening yellow-green glare. The visual refuge was no im-
provement. I, for one, couldn't tell which perception was
more unpleasant, the glaring yellow-green or the effect
of decay in the olive green.

After the initial shock, I braced myself, said goodnight

to my hosts and then proceeded to undress quickly so that I might put out the light as soon as possible. "Isn't it wonderful that there is no color without light." With this thought I pushed the electric switch.

When I awoke, a powerful glare from the east window and from the reflecting walls cut my eyes, and I found that I was soaked in perspiration and holding the headboard of my bed. I had had a nightmare. It was still in my memory, but it was not clear. I was in a huge barracks building with many men in uniform, thousands of men. The barracks were so long that you could not see the opposite end. I tried to see it, straining my eyes, but it was no use. I looked for a door, both at the left and at the right. There was no door, no way of getting out of this stifling place. It was terrifically hot; I was suffocating. I began to count the men that were in there with me. There were too many. I could not count them. I was choking for a long time. Suddenly, there appeared a large open space, not a door. The entire wall fell, and huge, powerful lights glared into my eyes. I was blinded and choking. I tried to escape. All at once I had an idea. I fell to the ground and rolled towards the lights. As I rolled and rolled, the lights kept cutting my eyes. I got hold of something. I stopped rolling, but my eyes were still in pain.

It was at this point I awoke in the unpleasant way described. The direct and reflected light glared into my eyes. I turned my gaze to the olive draperies. I felt like throwing up. I was nauseated.

I was glad to get out of bed. With relief I remembered that there was no chartreuse in the bathroom. It was in green-blue and made me feel cool and relaxed. Quite a change from what I had just been through!

When I walked into the living room, I saw the furnishings

in daylight for the first time. The light was subdued, and there was very little clear wall space. Therefore, although the drab, ornately framed pictures cluttering the walls were eyesores, the bilious yellow-green color was not apparent. At least, most visitors were not made uncomfortable by it.

Then I went into the dining room. The dining room walls were green-blue, as in the bathroom. The table and chairs were dark, heavy and loaded with gingerbread ornamentation. The blue upholstered seats and backs were obviously expensive. The blue floral-patterned rug was soft and also costly looking.

I tried to figure out what conscious or unconscious reason there might have been for having the same color in bathroom and dining room. "Lucky the dining room isn't chartreuse," I thought and gave up trying to determine common denominators.

I wandered into the kitchen and found the equipment attractive, modern, streamlined, trim and simple. The walls were blue, and the floor had linoleum in a pattern predominantly green. I wondered what my hostess imagined to be the connection between the green floor and the blue wall. Or was the color combination entirely accidental? Maybe she had just grown tired of the old color.

Perhaps she was bored. She couldn't change her husband; she couldn't change her children. It was not easy to change friends, and it probably would be a serious problem to move to another house. But colors, particularly wall colors, are always easy to change. They are no problem at all, especially if you can justify the change because the walls are soiled.

That was my last thought in silence because my hostess walked into the kitchen as I stood there in reflection. Then the master of the house and the two sons entered. My host and I took a walk and discussed business. When we returned, in about half an hour, breakfast was ready to be served.

At the breakfast table, I was asked how I had slept. Here was my cue to tell about my nightmare. "How do you interpret this terrible dream?" my hostess asked. "If you really want to know how I interpret it I will tell you," I said with alacrity. Both she and her husband insisted that I give them my analysis.

Since they had asked for it and I was sure they were my friends, I felt that they would understand that my motives were friendly, whether they agreed or disagreed with my interpretation.

I explained to them that apart from possible Freudian complications, the colors in the guest room were most likely responsible for setting off my nightmare. I pointed out that the yellow-green and olive green have low preference ratings, that few people like these two colors. I further explained that if only one of these were in the room, complemented by a violet, pure or grayed, it would not be so bad. The toned-down violet areas would relieve the vibrant effect. The violet areas would give the eyes a chance to rest before taking in the yellow-green waves again.

I observed that a color tone based on yellow-green, combined with grayed violet colors, could be a stimulating environment for some people, but that yellow-green, even with complementary colors, is not suitable for a guest room because it is liked by so few persons.

I explained why a bathroom should have a warm color, such as pink, and why a dining room should have "appetite colors" such as peach or raspberry. I further pointed out that blue and green ought not to be combined because they do not equal white light, are not natural pairs in human vision and do not provide a psychological balance of warm and cool colors.

There was silence as I spoke. Not even the young sons interrupted. Both my host and hostess were thoughtful for a number of minutes that seemed like a very long time. "I never realized there was so much to color," my hostess said at last in a dreamy voice. "Neither did I," my host added glumly. "We'll have to do something about it."

My hosts asked me for guidance. I prepared a color scheme for each room and took the liberty of citing some objectionable elements in the present furnishings. The entire house was redone by following and matching the color swatches I provided. The dark, ornate, overly heavy and clumsy looking furniture was sold at auction. Light wood pieces, simple and modern in style, replaced the old gingerbread-laden wood. Fresh-looking and colorful impressionist pictures replaced the drab prints and steel engravings.

Friends and acquaintances began calling this home "Harmony House," and a new problem came into being. So many people wanted to spend week ends at "Harmony House," where the company was always so gay and stimulating, that the proud and happy owners had to learn to schedule their entertainment. Week-end visits had to be arranged a month or more in advance.

"We will never forget what you have done for us," said my hostess with much feeling and sincerity. "It's downright amazing," added my host, "to see what difference the right colors can make."

More than any other single experience, this episode was responsible for my decision to devote my time and effort to giving color guidance to the homemaker as well as to the business executive. I wanted to repeat thousands of times the satisfying experience that my hosts had had by color-tuning their home scientifically. I realize that millions of good, intelligent, cultured people use color haphazardly and need guidance in creating the surroundings that promote happiness.

10. What Colors Should a Brunette Have in Her Room?

Brunettes look best against a background of warm, light colors derived from the yellow, orange and red families. Beige, cocoa, peach and tan provide favorable contrast for the brunette. Light- and medium-toned greens also provide sufficient contrast. Deep blue should be avoided.

If you are a brunette and are striving to emphasize that point, the background in your room may be either light in tone or else rich and vibrant. You should avoid grays and extremely deep tones.

You can afford to have vibrant surroundings. Whereas a blonde would lose by a strong background, you can gain. Actually, your hair will have contrast against any color except one that is very deep in value.

If your furniture is limed oak, bleached mahogany or some other light colored wood, you should avoid a delicate or light tone for your walls and should choose a rich, vibrant tint or tone. If your wood pieces are dark, you are free if you wish to use a delicate or light tone on the walls.

With rich-toned or brilliant color on your walls, deep-toned or pure white accents are highly effective, and a piece of sculpture in ebony or white will contribute much to the interior. If the walls are brilliant in color, a pair of contrasting black-and-white photos will enrich the room effectively. With walls nearly neutral in tone, a water-color or oil painting (original or reproduction) in brilliant colors will make the best contribution.

Draperies, in either a pure hue for light- or neutral-toned walls or a deep tone for vibrant-colored walls, will frame the window properly. If the walls are rose, deep green draperies will be ideal. For peach walls, turquoise draperies may be used. Green walls and wine-red draperies make an effective combination.

For a room with rose walls you may have a deep wine-red or raspberry-red rug, since all three colors are based on the same red hue. You may also have a green rug which is complementary to rose. Always, as in the case of other rooms, the rug may be either related or complementary to the color of the walls.

To emphasize that you are a brunette, always remember to avoid a dark background. Otherwise, choose colors primarily for your psychological needs.

Brunettes can be exotic, and if you are striving for a striking effect, use light values derived from a magenta red in your room. If you don't care for an overstimulating effect, avoid reds and provide for yourself a background of light delicate tones derived from yellow or orange with a few accessories in rich complementary and related colors.

11. What Colors Should You Have If You Are Brown-Haired?

If you have brown hair and are of medium complexion, you are free to go on an emotional binge as far as color is concerned. Either warm or cool colors will provide contrast. You should make your color choice on the basis of getting emotional satisfaction and meeting the physical conditions of your room. The colors of the rainbow are before you to serve your purpose.

With brown hair and a medium skin color you are less likely to be conscious of what color can do for your appearance and more conscious of what it can do for your emotions. Blondes and redheads are often preoccupied with their hair, but the brown-haired are rarely exhibitionistic about this feature. They are, therefore, free to choose color primarily on a psychological or emotional basis, whereas blondes and redheads might hesitate to surround themselves with exotic backgrounds.

If you wish to provide for yourself a rich and vibrant environment, you may use red and green combinations in a pure or toned-down state. You may have a red couch or red draperies or both. If you do enjoy the stimulating reds, if they pep you up, why not use them? Then, of course, your greens should be more calm in tone. Light green tones will provide relief from the vibrant reds. Your eyes will need the relief. Your nervous system will profit from the soft, subtle areas of green.

You may have brilliant ceramics, brilliantly colored pictures and bright draperies against walls of rose, peach, green or blue. Of course, the colors should be complementaries. However, you should avoid using two colors that are pure complementaries on the large areas in your room. Pure complementaries in large areas are not stimulating but irritating; they are too rich. Because they are too vibrant, they are not suitable for a room which is to be lived in.

12. What Colors Should a Redhead Have in Her Room?

If you are a redhead you scintillate in the green-blue fields, in the verdant park, in the summer garden. Green-blue is your background color. Green-blue, being the complementary to orange-red, makes the red more vibrant and attractive. A titian-haired miss should never be found against a red background. Red detracts from titian-colored hair and makes it rusty-looking.

Cool green-blues are ideal for your walls. If you have no deep-seated, unconscious dislike for cerulean or cyan, try using it pure and in nearly full strength on the wall of your room. Your hair will vibrate against it. The green-blue will make you look most attractive.

As accents, do not use the complementary orange-red in the pure state. Use a shade of orange-red that approaches a chocolate color. The deep chocolate brown is preferable because it will not compete with your hair. If you are proud of your titian-colored hair, you will want nothing in your room to vibrate but your hair. Therefore, in your room you should avoid brilliant warm reds entirely. Have instead green-blues in many shades, tints and tones, including the most brilliant green-blue.

The rug may be either a deep brown or green-blue. A cool green-blue tone is generally more appealing to feminine taste. A man is more likely to be satisfied with brown.

The drapery for the window may be either a light tone or a deep shade based on orange-red. It may have a pattern, incorporating both deep and light tones. Other accessories such as ceramics should be dark brown, deep green-blue or white to contrast with the pure green-blue of the walls. Remember that although white in large areas is optically and psychologically negative, small spots or objects of white are effective accents.

13. What Colors Should a Blonde Have in Her Room?

If you have blonde hair, blue or violet-blue is your color, for if your goal is to complement your blonde hair a blue background will do it for you. If you have no deep-seated unconscious aversion to blue or violet-blue you will naturally be drawn to that color.

You may use a deep violet-blue tone on the wall if you have light-colored furniture and sufficient light in your room. Also, you should be aware that a fully saturated violet-blue is highly exotic, and therefore you may find a deep tone of violet-blue to be a little too strong.

A medium tone of violet-blue on the walls is generally most satisfactory with either light or dark furniture because it will provide sufficient contrast for either. Better still, the color will not absorb too much of the light.

As accessories, use a yellow and/or olive color (yellow plus black) related to the color of your hair. These spots will give the violet-blue tone more life by complementary contrast. You may want a few small objects in brilliant yellow, but most of the colors should be neutral because pure yellow may give your hair considerable competition.

The draperies should be of a predominantly yellow-based tone. A pattern of olive green and violet-blue on a yellow or ivory background would be ideal. Such a color pattern would not vibrate or stand out too much against the wall color, yet there would be sufficient contrast for framing the window. The rug could be a grayed violet-blue or a yellow-ish tone, such as beige or tan.

14. What Colors Should the Mature White-Haired Person Have in Her Room?

White or gray hair is neutral and looks its best against a brilliantly colored background. If you are mature enough to have silvery hair and are not too inhibited, nervous or moody, you will enjoy a brilliantly colored setting.

Why not rich or exotic colors on the walls? If you have many highly colorful pictures, you will of course want a neutral background for these. If the pictures on your walls are black and white, you can get stimulation from color on the walls.

If you have no aversion to colors of the red family, put a dusty rose on the walls, combined with rich green draperies and a light-toned green rug. This will be a wonderful setting. A few red ceramics will provide additional eye stimulus.

Primarily, you will consider your psychological needs in choosing the dominant color for your walls. If you need much stimulation, choose a dominant color from the red family. If you need calming, you will be much better off with a cool background color such as delicate blue or a gray-blue tone.

However, remember that accompanying colors should be determined on the basis of physical laws, optical principles and psychological effect. This means that after you have decided on the background or dominant color, you should consult the charts (the chart from which it was selected and the chart with which that chart forms a pair) for the other colors. Keep in mind that each pair of charts gives you a choice of fifty colors, all based on a pair of complementary hues.

Remember also that if the furniture is dark, you will need a light color on the walls. If the furniture is light, you may have a deep tone on the walls, provided that your illumination is sufficient. If your natural light is limited, it will be a mistake to have deep-toned walls.

With your white hair you have the satisfaction of knowing that you will look attractive against any color. In your room, indulge yourself in color, get the most of the psychological possibilities from your surroundings. Appropriate colors will give you much happiness.

If you are mature enough to have white hair you have settled down to being yourself and expressing yourself— you probably have more freedom now to do the things you enjoy than at any other period in your life. By all means, now is the time, of all times, to make color do things for you.

Get brilliant colors in your furnishings—draperies, couches and chairs. Get a few ceramic and sculpture pieces to use as accents. They, too, will contribute to the enrichment of your life. Watch the favorable effect a brilliant background will have on other people's attitudes toward you. Surround yourself with vibrant colors to dramatize your white hair, to help yourself feel young in spirit.

CHAPTER THREE

Psychological and Social Factors in Color and Design Preferences

1. Conditioned Color Reactions

The first chapter was devoted primarily to effects of using color properly and improperly. In the second chapter, I showed how to color-tune each room in a typical home. In this chapter, I should like you to see more clearly why one chooses certain colors, enjoying some and rejecting others.

Again, I must make it clear, as I did once before, that a great deal of research is still to be done on the psychological aspects of color. In this area I am therefore content to give you chiefly the benefit of my experience in conducting tests at Color Research Institute. Above all, I mean to avoid highly technical language and use plain talk that you can understand without resorting to a dictionary of psychology and philosophy.

We may surmise that since babies and adults of primitive societies, such as African natives, love red, the love for red is ingrained in human nature. But how about the preference for pink? Mother loves pink, but baby does not. Neither does the primitive adult. This must mean that the enjoyment of pink is acquired. In other words, there are two kinds of color preferences, instinctive and acquired. How are the preferences acquired?

And why is it that no color has complete acceptance? Magenta red, for example, is liked by more than 90 per cent of all people. How about those few who don't like the color, even in a small quantity, as found in a tie or a blouse? And what makes a few people enjoy a color that the majority can't tolerate? These elements have been touched upon in the first two chapters; now let us look further into the psychological and sociological factors in our color preferences and learn why these factors are often so powerful that they submerge what might be termed natural feelings and reactions.

From psychoanalysis we learn that only a small proportion of the individual's total experience (or emotional life) is within his conscious grasp. Some of an individual's experiences can be recalled by casual association and some by special techniques, but a good part remains forever beyond the reach of his conscious mind.

We generally recognize that much of our past has been

forgotten. But more difficult to accept is the knowledge that these experiences are not really lost but remain in the unconscious where they continue to exert tremendous power over our behavior.

Our overt actions, therefore, are often dictated by forces hidden deep in the unconscious. Unconscious motivations rather than reasoning generally determine how an individual will behave.

Human behavior is conditioned by habit, and habit is as regular in its pattern as is a set of gears and wheels driven by a motor. Evidence that behavior patterns are formed through habit and association has been most effectively brought out, as is well known, by J. P. Pavlov, the Russian scientist, author of the theory of the "conditioned reflex." The theory is based on very extensive experiments with dogs.

Pavlov regularly gave a dog a piece of meat immediately after the ringing of a bell. The association of the bell-ringing and the meat-eating was repeated until after a certain period of time the ringing of the bell without the meat produced a flow of saliva in the mouth of the dog. The bell and the meat produced identical reactions. Thus is formed a "conditioned reflex."

However, "conditioned reflexes" can be inhibited or changed. If, after a dog has been conditioned to associate the ringing of a bell with eating meat, the bell continues to be rung but is followed repeatedly either by no meat or by some painful treatment, the saliva soon ceases to flow. This is an "inhibitory reflex," which, if allowed to confuse the dog too often, can lead to neurotic symptoms.

Human beings are conditioned from infancy by their environment. The conditioning is neither voluntary nor conscious. A new-born child acts freely and instinctively. If we do not interfere with the infant's spontaneous behavior but gratify his natural needs for food and fondling (love), the infant may grow up to be extremely self-indulgent, egotistic and antisocial, but he will not be in danger of becoming an inhibited individual. However, in order to make the child conform to family or group behavior patterns, the parents begin to inhibit the infant by restricting his spontaneous behavior, and therein lies some danger—the possibility of the child's pathological withdrawal from his environment into himself.

Excessive inhibition is the road to neurosis. Normally, there is a near balance between self-expression and inhibition. The less inhibited individual is familiarly called an extrovert, the overly inhibited person, an introvert. Most people are an admixture of extrovert and introvert characteristics.

Normally, you are at the height of happiness when you can express yourself freely—that is, when you are not obliged to undertake a conscious repression or when you need not strain to control your emotional life. However, you and your neighbor are likely to infringe upon each other if you both insist upon unlimited freedom of expression. Hence we are all necessarily inhibited to some degree, first by the family and then by society. In other words, normal people have dual behavior patterns, comprising a network of reactions that are "instinctive" or "unconditioned" (original, libidinous) and those which are conditioned and inhibited.

We know that the liking for red is about as spontaneous as any preference can be. A negative reaction to black is equally "unrehearsed." However, a person can be conditioned both to avoid red and to react pleasurably to black.

Suppose each time that red is put before a new-born child it is accompanied or followed by a pin prick or other type of painful experience: the child will almost certainly grow up with a strong dislike for red.

On the other hand, suppose a new-born infant is given food and continuously fondled by the mother only in the dark—never when there is light. Black or dark will then become associated with enjoyable experiences. This child, in other words, will become conditioned to react to black with pleasure.

Since mothers don't make a practice of pricking their infants with pins and generally prefer to sleep at night and feed and fondle their babies in the daytime, people are ordinarily left undisturbed in their normal attraction to red and negative feeling about black.

Those people who have been conditioned to an active dislike of red are generally much inhibited. Some unconsciously associate the vibrant red with immorality, while perhaps rationalizing their aversion or "inhibitory reflex" as a mark of "good taste."

Originally, when Puritanism was a ruling social force, the linking of red with moral looseness was on a conscious level. We are reminded of such associations as the "scarlet letter." Red was deliberately frowned upon as a symbol of sensuality and sin. Nowadays this association is no longer openly avowed. A dislike for or negative reaction to red, although probably due in most cases to a hang-over of the Puritan tradition, is hardly ever traced directly to sexual taboos.

The conditioning you received from the day of your birth has undoubtedly played its part in molding your color preferences. This fact should always be kept in mind when you are called upon to make a choice of colors for yourself or for others.

2. Ego-Involvement, Prestige Identification and Your Libido

Individuals are not emotionally involved with such products as detergents. However, they are emotionally involved with their wearing apparel and their home furnishings. Planning your home involves three types of powerful motivations —ego-involvement, prestige identification and libido.

Your self-esteem and self-respect, your individuality and the development of your personality are all elements of ego-involvement. Your attempt at identification with a leading group, your desire to be in fashion and to keep up with the Joneses, are prestige identification. The libido may be roughly defined as the pleasure drive, the urge to self-indulgence or the craving for unhampered emotional and physical expression.

Frequently ego-involvement and prestige identification are closely related to each other but may not always be in harmony with libidinous drives. To feel self-important as a result of identification with the "best people" may not be conducive to your pleasure in life if the behavior of the "best people" is opposed at all points to your idea of fun. In that case the demands of your libido come into conflict with what you consider your other strong needs, and you may have a major psychological problem on your hands.

In the normal individual, the basic components of personality are fairly well balanced. Whatever conflicts arise are solved without much strain on the psychological make-up. Some individuals, indeed, are exceptionally well adjusted or integrated and take all difficulties in their stride. Others, on the contrary, find trouble and turmoil wherever they turn. Such unhappy persons are referred to as neurotic or emotionally unbalanced.

The following case of a young lady in a women's wear shop illustrates how reactions to colors may bare emotional conflict. The miss told the saleswoman that one of the dress designs fitted her perfectly, as though it had been designed for her figure. The dress was available in four colors—coral, fuchsia, turquoise and chartreuse. The young lady had no use for the coral. But she found it difficult to make up her mind between the fuchsia, a color she had been told flattered her complexion, the chartreuse, which was featured in a leading fashion magazine and the turquoise, which she considered the most beautiful color. In her attitude toward the turquoise and the coral she was reacting in terms of likes and dislikes; in the case of the fuchsia and chartreuse she was conscious that the first would enhance her appearance and that the second would cause people to consider her in fashion.

Assuming the young lady was able to buy only one dress, which did she choose? This depended on the type of person she was. If she was an especially self-confident and independent person who did not care much about the opinions of others, she chose the turquoise blue, which she liked as a color. If she felt self-conscious about her complexion and wanted to improve it, she selected the fuchsia. If she was primarily concerned about social recognition and was particularly concerned with fashion, she most likely purchased the chartreuse, even if otherwise she felt quite indifferent to this color.

The young lady was exhibiting conflict between three

contending motives. The fuchsia flattered her complexion; this effect was therefore an element of ego-involvement. The chartreuse was in fashion and thus represented prestige identification. The turquoise dress she felt was beautiful. Her emotions dictated this preference, so turquoise was the favorite color on a libidinous basis.

Marketing research showed that only about 20 per cent of women shopping for clothes chose colors because of personal fondness for them. About 40 per cent made their choices because they wished to enhance their complexions, and the remaining 40 per cent took the colors that were currently in fashion. Apparently in a matter of this kind, the majority of women are more concerned with ego-involvement and prestige identification than with indulgence in personal pleasure.

Prestige identification is often unconscious. Individuals are not always aware that the reason they want period furniture is because it is associated with social status. Consciously they may believe they really feel comfortable with highly ornate wallpapers and tapestries and elaborately carved woodwork. They may actually persuade themselves that they enjoy these types of home furnishings. The sense of importance that comes from association with anything pertaining to the great of the past often compensates for the lack of relaxation resulting from a gingerbread environment. Thus people may suppress their natural or instinctive feelings and substitute satisfactions derived from prestige identification and glorification of the ego.

Where individuals are ostentatious, "ego-involvement" is synonymous with "prestige identification." Expensive-looking period furniture and gaudy pseudo-modernistic furniture are often bought because of the desire to show wealth and to emphasize the thought, "I can afford it; I am a success; I live like a king." "I" means the ego. "Living like a king" means prestige identification.

However, the pleasure drive or the libido is not so easily defeated. In the purchase of clothing, for example, strong personal color preferences are apt to win out.

I know a young lady who explained her purchase of two sweaters as follows: "I really love my shocking pink sweater, but I bought the yellow one also because everybody is wearing yellow. It's in style." The next three weeks saw her wearing the pink sweater nine times, the yellow one twice.

Another woman of my acquaintance bought two coats, one "because they are wearing blue this season," another because she likes beige. The following month she wore the beige coat twenty-one times to three times for the blue coat.

The pink sweater and the beige coat will soon need replacement. The yellow and the blue garments will remain hanging in the closet, a constant reminder of bad purchases.

You can't very well buy furniture that way. You are not likely to have one living room because you enjoy it and another because it's in fashion, nor is it probable that you will have one bedroom for your own use and another for impressing your friends.

To derive the greatest possible benefit from your home, I suggest that you gratify your emotional cravings first and put other considerations second. Be yourself! Indulge yourself within reason, and do not be overly concerned with what others think. Fashion as such is a false god. And since motives of ego-involvement and prestige identification are often unconscious, you will do well to examine yourself rather carefully before planning your furnishings.

3. Phobias and Fetishes—Do You Have Any?

Occasionally you meet a person who has a fear of or an aversion to a specific color. We have reason to believe that any such strong feeling has its roots in a traumatic experience associated with the color in question. An association of this sort should not be confused with a normally negative attitude toward a color or with rejection of a color for a specific purpose. For example, you would not want orange for your living-room wall because it would be too vibrant and too stimulating. That does not mean that you wouldn't buy oranges for your breakfast or that you would walk out of someone else's room because it had orange walls. On the other hand, if you associated orange with pain in your unconscious, you might react in just those ways. You would get your vitamin C from other sources than oranges, and you would flee in horror from any walls or other large areas decked out in the detested color.

I received a report of a man who had a green phobia—a relatively rare affliction, much less common than phobias to red, blue or yellow. He despised anything green. He would not go to a park. He remained in his room as much as he could. He conducted his business and did his work as a mechanic at his home so that he wouldn't have to see grass and trees on the way to work. Needless to say, there was no foliage on his property.

An individual personally known to me had an olive-green phobia. He would not eat olives, and when he met a soldier in an olive-green uniform, he would avert his eyes. At a dinner table with this individual, who was in his early fifties, I attempted to discover the origin of his olive-green complex.

He first claimed he had always hated olive-green, but in answer to my carefully phrased questions, he soon admitted that he had undergone a combination of unfortunate experiences in connection with that color. He had been poisoned by tainted food of an olive-green color, and he had been placed under the strain of seeing hardly anything but olive-green uniforms and faded grass for weeks at a time during his service in World War I. He told of other disagreeable incidents in similar vein. When he had finished, there was little doubt in my mind how certain unhappy events in his past had helped to bring out his phobia, even though there were probably deeper implications in his case.

There are individuals who have an abnormally strong attraction to a specific color. There are many who love any color as long as it is of the red family. Others are partial to blue. Still others have a veritable obsession for riotous combinations. The man I described as detesting olive-green always wore bright ties. When I commented on his taste one day, he replied somewhat astonishingly, "I love bright color. I wish I could wear red, blue and yellow suits and get away with it. Maybe I wouldn't even care what anyone said, if I could afford to get them custom-made in those colors."

One young woman in her twenties had a passion for navy blue. Her clothes were all navy blue. She wore navy blue suits or dresses to the office, and on social occasions her favorite costume was a beautifully cut navy blue evening gown adorned with a gold sash. It was at a party, where she was escorted by a young man in a navy blue suit, that I first began to suspect a fetish.

Soon afterward I had dinner at her home (her three rooms were furnished in blue and white, with numerous brass lamps), and learned that she had had an ill-fated love affair with a navy man, killed while she had been visiting him. Apparently navy blue had become a symbol of her lost love.

Curiously, she was reluctant to admit her obvious devotion to this color. When I somewhat disingenuously asked her to tell me her favorite hues, she named white and yellow! Perhaps she was self-conscious and sensitive on the subject of blue.

Some individuals feel an abnormally strong attraction for colors with low preference ratings, that is, for colors which are unpopular.

I met one such person, an elderly woman, in the diner of a train. Her fetish was olive-green—the very color that drove my friend in the bright ties to distraction. She wore an olive-green suit, an olive-green blouse, an olive-green hat. Her shoes were of greenish leather. What attracted my attention, however, was not so much her attire, which looked like that of the Women's Army Corps, although more feminine in style, as her ordering of a third serving of green olives.

I began a conversation with her and found her an intelligent, well-traveled person. She had been to Paris, so I started talking about art exhibits and Paris fashions. This led to color. I asked her which she thought were the best colors for decorating a room. "Olive is luscious," she assured me.

"Do you think I should use it for my study?" I asked.

"I think olive is just wonderful for a study," she gushed. "My room is olive-green. I simply adore it. It's really my bedroom, but I call it my olive room. I couldn't find olive draperies, so I had them specially dyed in the right color."

She seemed entirely oblivious of anything unusual in her monomania. In color, as in politics, I mused, passions can run high. And what is one person's phobia may be another person's fetish.

4. The Psychology of Black, White and Gray

Black may be psychologically termed a depressant. It rates very low in preference. Traditionally, it is associated with death, and optically, as it reflects no light, it is a perfect negative.

Nevertheless, although black is seldom liked for itself, it plays an important role of negation; it makes adjacent colors more vibrant and more beautiful, and it has a narrowing effect that may be highly useful.

You choose your black gown not because you love black but because it sets off the color and form you wish to display. Framed against a black gown, your complexion looks richer, and in black your figure appears more slender. These enhancing and slimming effects of black are well known.

If your husband buys black lingerie for you on your birthday or wedding anniversary, he is probably aware of the foregoing facts. He loves you and wants to see you look your best. However, if he enjoys looking at black for its own sake, perhaps to the extent of ordering the walls of his room painted black, it is time to call a psychiatrist. Something is seriously wrong.

A small black table may serve a purpose basically similar to that of a black gown. You may wish to use such a table for displaying a ceramic, a piece of sculpture or some other object.

Like black, white is not psychologically satisfying when used by itself in large areas. It reflects too much light and has an irritating, glaring impact upon the eye. However, white, too, enhances other colors. It makes adjacent colors more appealing, not by contrast, but by illumination.

To some people white is a symbol of purity, virginity or

merely clean or sanitary surroundings. Those who enjoy great expanses of white are apt to be rather repressed individuals.

An expressed liking for gray amounts to an evasion. Gray does not specify a hue. It is half white and half black. To say, therefore, "I like gray" is to say, in effect, "I won't tell you the color I really love." A man who tells you that this is his favorite color may mean simply that gray makes him look most conservative or dignified. Actually he may secretly enjoy brilliant red or bright blue.

Of course a person could withhold information on his color preferences by saying that he likes blue when he really favors red. It is not that people will deliberately lie about this subject: they are often unconscious of their hidden cravings; they may be inhibited; they may have conflicting feelings or they may be confused by ego-involvement and prestige identification. It is thus hazardous to try to arrive at sound judgments about personality on the basis of expressed color preferences.

5. Wallpaper: Its Psychological Aspect

There is a place in the home for certain types of wallpaper. In the nursery, wallpapers with designs of animals —puppies, kittens and bunnies—are appropriate. Such wallpapers should be hung as murals, and they should be changed every six months in order to enrich the child's knowledge of the animal world. Children get much pleasure from the animal pictures. A wallpaper mural of bird subjects, butterflies and fish is very stimulating to young children. The mural should be no wider than one width of wallpaper because too many elaborate designs and acrobatic figures are often overstimulating to children.

To use the animal-motif wallpapers for any other room except the nursery can have only one or more of the following meanings: that you were sold a bill of goods because you couldn't say no to a salesman; that you have a primitive taste for images; that you have a suppressed desire for fishing and hunting; or that you are still somewhat child-like in your attitude toward the animal world. Similarly, a choice of floral patterns for your large spaces may mean that you are starved for flowers and greenery for which the wall decoration serves as a rather pathetic "ersatz."

The latest abomination is Chinese wallpaper or wallpaper depicting Chinese or Japanese women (really courtesans) and pagodas. If you have been sold one of these wallpapers it may mean that you have a strong desire to travel to strange, distant lands. Since you can't do that, you compensate by bringing a little of the dream wish into the home in the form of wallpaper.

Such unconscious compensations should not be taken lightly. If you don't know when to say no, it means that you have an inner wish to say yes, only you need to be encouraged. In these circumstances, a good salesman will easily brush aside your token sales resistance.

Examine yourself critically before you succumb to the lure of filling the interior of your home with floral monstrosities and red-coated hunters. Once you have unearthed the existence of hidden urges within yourself, once you have found out that pagodas and butterflies on the wall are paper compensations for inner yearnings, you will enjoy the discovery as a joke and reject the razzle-dazzle wallpapers as artistic and psychological frauds. You will begin to treat walls as walls, colors as colors, designs as designs; as for the wish to see distant lands, you may be able to take that trip after all or decide to gratify your wanderlust by reading travel books.

To sum up: A wallpaper pattern portraying animal or fairy-tale scenes is excellent for the baby's room if it is hung as a picture panel or mural. Elsewhere it, together with all cheap and gaudy styles, is out of place. To live daily with atrocities on the walls can do more harm than is generally believed possible—as I have tried to show throughout this book.

Of course, not all wallpaper for grown-ups is to be condemned. If you are fond of this type of decoration, you can easily find subtle patterns and colors that may be used in place of paint for creating a favorable background.

6. Functional Design and Your Emotions

Traditional concepts would have us believe that aesthetic elements are separate from utilitarian factors. Many people still regard aesthetic values as frills, entirely divorced from functional realities. However, there is a growing realization that the beauty and utility of an article often react upon each other—that proper design envisages not only the practical factor of performance but also the aesthetic factor of appearance.

In modern eyes, function is usually closely related to aesthetic design. For example, the principle of streamlining gives the automobile and the airplane additional speed as well as beauty. And in furniture, psychological effect, no less than physical character, is a factor in design.

The primary function of a chair is to be sat in. Anything that contributes to the comfort of sitting in the chair adds to its functional value. The modern chair of simplified design is smooth and spacious and therefore is most functional, whereas narrow traditional lines inconvenience the sitter and decrease the functional value of the chair.

The secondary purpose of a chair is to be pleasing to the eye. Modern furniture design is simple and passive in character. It is unobtrusive and produces an atmosphere of restfulness.

In a simpler society, intricacy in the home was an important psychological counterweight to an uneventful milieu. Elaborate, highly stimulating interior designs balanced the tranquil social and business life in the outside world. Fine, embroidered linens, multicolored rugs, ornate decorations all served a definite psychological purpose.

Many of us still look upon unnecessarily complex design as beautiful because we continue to think with "craft minds"; that is, our ideas are still dominated by craft standards, even though the Industrial Revolution started generations ago. But in a technological society such as ours, intricate and multicolored decorations have no place. They have no psychological relationship to the tempo and character of modern life. For better or for worse, we live in an era of synthetic materials, streamlined machines and huge industrial plants geared to mass production. In such an environment, simplicity of form and pattern inevitably characterize aesthetic as well as industrial standards.

Then again, because modern life is fast and full of turmoil, the present-day home should be mainly a place for rest and relaxation. After bearing up all day under countless strains and stresses, we are glad to go home to relax. And we relax best in surroundings of soft colors and simple forms.

The radio and television can be turned on or off at will. Dramatic pictures on the walls may be admired, ignored or even removed, depending on our mood. But we cannot shut off or avoid the impressions created by the colors and furnishings of a room in which we spend hours at a time. Blazing floral patterns, intricately carved woodwork, chairs and tables that defy relaxation—these are not the ingredients of a restful atmosphere.

What we must have, if we are to live in a home in which we can restore our energies, is an environment properly color-tuned and functionally harmonious. The furniture should be passive in form, with smooth, soft, inviting lines. It should be unobtrusive, not irritating or fatiguing to the eye. It should not make us apprehensive of bruising ourselves on sharp corners or of sitting on thorny roses of dazzling upholstery.

Modern furniture, free from limiting conceptions in design, is comfortable. Being easily and quickly cleaned, it is adapted to the smoky, sooty conditions of present-day cities. Lacking ornate, frilly patterns, it is an aid to relaxation, one of the chief psychological and physical needs of our times.

A thoroughly mischievous notion is that there are two kinds of art, the functional and the decorative. "Fine" art is not supposed to be useful; the term "functional" is interpreted in the narrowest possible sense as contributing to nothing but bare physical survival.

The absurdity of this view becomes evident when we reflect that it would relegate dress design and architecture even beyond the functional category on the grounds that animal skins and caves are sufficient to provide man with warmth and shelter.

The fact is, of course, that man does not "live by bread alone." He has a wide variety of needs, physical, intellectual, aesthetic, emotional and spiritual. Anything that meets these needs is "functional." Color is as functional as a steam boiler.

In feudal and aristocratic periods, when useful work was regarded as degrading, the game of inventing unreal distinctions between the "fine" and the "practical" served to justify the "gentleman's" existence. In our democratic society, we are all ladies and gentlemen—and most of us are workers, too. We have no use for semantic nonsense. All arts are fine; all arts are practical. The chef is as much concerned with the taste of the food as with the nourishment it provides. Houses are not built merely for the purpose of protecting people from cold and rain. In the design of refrigerators and automatic washers, artists have their say along with engineers.

Emotional and aesthetic needs in our society are met not only by music, painting and other traditionally "fine" arts (which are as indispensable to many of us as meat and bread) but also by modern industrial design, with its simple, restful and graceful lines.

7. Should You Get Modern Furniture?

The answer to this question should already have become obvious to you from the preceding discussion of functional design. One might as well ask whether you should get a modern cooking range, a modern refrigerator, a telephone.

Getting modern furniture for a modern interior is just a matter of providing yourself with simple forms, smooth lines and harmonious colors in preference to angular, ornate, elaborate, uncomfortable and eye-straining anachronisms. Why punish your nervous system?

Let me emphasize at this point that by modern furniture I mean only furniture that is simple, restful and unobtrusive.

Not all furniture that is called (or miscalled) modern is pleasing in this functional sense. Some contemporaneous designs are akin to the most ornate and ostentatious period styles.

Fine modern furniture incorporates new materials, new designs, new construction techniques and a more advanced knowledge of color, all of which are inspired by and geared to functional concepts.

Your grandparents had period furniture with elaborate carvings and traceries. Perhaps they also had servants to take care of it or else many children to help with the housework. You, most likely, are not blessed with either a staff of servants or a dozen children to do your cleaning for you. Surely you have a better use for your time than chasing dirt around curlicues and scrolls in period chairs. That is why you have, or hope to get, all the modern automatic household equipment you can, and that is why you need modern easy-on-the-eyes and easy-to-take-care-of furniture.

"Why did I even dream that I wanted traditional furniture?" you may ask yourself after you have thought about furniture rationally. The reason probably goes back to your early childhood. People often have a way of unconsciously associating pleasant experiences in the past with bygone surroundings. If you were brought up in a happy home with baroque interior decoration, you are likely to keep a warm spot in your heart for baroque furnishings.

Perhaps you feel a nostalgic yearning, a desire to escape into the past. Period furniture and antiques may then symbolize the "good old days." Factors such as these may never rise fully into consciousness, or if they do, may not long preoccupy you, but yet may be powerful enough to thwart a decision to do away with the irritations and inefficiencies of out-dated interiors.

Another reason why some people want to hang on to traditional furniture is simply that they are too lazy to modernize their outlook. They are the victims of inertia, the slaves of early indoctrination. They consciously and deliberately object to all and any change. "What was good enough for my folks is good enough for me" is their familiar refrain. So they sit tight and never have the least notion of how they might be benefited by a fresh idea, a revivifying experience, a new horizon.

Lastly there are the self-important ones whom we have already described. They get Louis XV furnishings because these are associated with the Bourbon Court. They get Neo-classic pieces that can be traced to the heroic days of Napoleon. Consciously or otherwise, they wish to identify themselves with the great of the past; they feel happy only if they can shine in reflected glory. No doubt all this is rather childish, but who is to say them nay if such things give them pleasure?

The point for you to bear in mind is that if you share none of these foibles or if you succeed in overcoming any that you may have, you will no more tolerate your ancestors' furniture and color schemes than you would copy their laundry methods, their lighting systems or their modes of transportation. Not because modern furniture and harmonious colors are in style, but because they will add to your happiness—that, I'm sure you will agree, is a rational reason for surrounding yourself with the finest products of modern skill and knowledge.

8. Pictures, Sculpture and Ceramics for the Home

Pictures are among the most important elements in a home. They make ideal accents. They are factors in determining the character of a room. Pictures should be placed on the walls in relation to the room arrangement. If a wall is to produce the maximum favorable effect in the interior scheme, it should be composed as if it were a picture itself.

What kind of pictures should you have? Modern, traditional, abstract, realistic, romantic, impressionist, expressionist? Are you going to buy "decorator pictures" or works of art? Will you get originals or reproductions?

Whether you should have modern or traditional pictures should be determined by the type of furniture you have. If the room is furnished in traditional style, by all means have traditional pictures. That is, select pictures of the same character as your furniture.

Whether your pictures should be original paintings or reproductions depends primarily on your financial status. Aesthetically, a fine and accurate reproduction is no less effective than the original. But there are other elements in art besides the aesthetic, such as ego-involvement and economic value. An original work of art by an old master gives satisfaction chiefly because it is the only one of its kind and carries a commensurate price tag, thus stamping the owner as a person of wealth and culture.

So-called "decorator pictures" are generally monstrosities that are sold to people who have not taken the time or made the effort to learn something about art. Like certain wallpaper designs, this type of picture usually consists of badly painted florals, gilded birds or Chinese women (courtesans) in Japanese robes. They are neither emotionally nor intellectually satisfying. They are psychological irritants. Their presence in a home betrays a lack of appreciation of art values and often mirrors mental sterility and emotional stagnation of the occupants. Anyone who has been sold pictures of this type would do well to throw them out as quickly as possible and replace them with fine reproductions of genuine art.

The fact that you have this book in your hand automatically takes you out of the class that would be satisfied with the so-called "decorator pictures." If you enjoy flowers, you will want real flowers or a picture of flowers by an artist who loves and understands them and knows how to paint them. If you love birds, you will want a live bird or paintings by an artist whose work compares with that of Audubon who both understood and knew how to portray birds. His birds aren't gilded.

If your furniture is modern, you will of course want modern pictures. Modern furniture is simple in line and form. It is light in color. The pictures should express the same characteristics of simplicity, lightness and airiness. Whether your pictures are abstract, realistic or impressionist depends on your personal taste, education and temperament.

For that matter, your furniture itself is a matter of personal choice. The only thing to keep in mind is that the pictures should harmonize with the essential character of the furniture.

If you want a little of the "ego satisfaction" that comes from having a work of art that no one else can have, be on the lookout for young, talented painters. Generally, if you make an offer of a fairly moderate sum for a water color, the young artist will accept. After all, a sensible painter who is setting out on a career wants to distribute his works as quickly as he can and keep on painting new ones. Water colors may be obtained in this way for about the same price commanded by good reproductions of works by internationally famous artists.

With a little study and experience, you will learn to judge creative art. You will gradually develop the ability to recognize an artist's technique and style. You may finally become expert in picking the artist with the most promising future and thus get works that are good investments as well as aesthetically satisfying.

One way of getting paintings for your home is to produce them yourself. Join an art class. Read books on the subject. Study the fundamentals of painting, and learn the joys of expressing yourself with brush and palette. To make sure that the colors of your art work will harmonize with the hues of your walls and furnishings (an important point covered below in the paragraphs on color in pictures as an integral part of the surroundings), consult the color charts in this book before you set out to paint.

You will not immediately produce masterpieces. For a while your technique may be weak; your efforts may lack spontaneity and originality. But keep at it. Watch your growth. You will develop skill and power. And you'll feel a glow of satisfaction when at last you can hang on your walls something you, yourself have created—comparing not unfavorably perhaps with the works of artists already represented in the home.

In buying pictures, even more important to consider than the artist, style, technique or school of art are the colors. Pictures should be a harmonious part of the interior. The colors in the pictures should be coordinated with those in the draperies, upholstered furniture and rug.

An ideal picture is one that incorporates and concentrates the complementary colors of the interior. At least the large, important picture in the room should display these complementary colors. Other colors, of course, may be present in small spots.

A room that has a delicate gray-green rug, deep green chairs and a red sofa should have a picture with predominantly pure, rich, vibrant greens and reds. In this case, it would be a mistake to have a picture with, say, predominantly violet-blue and yellow colors, as these would be an optical and psychological irritant in a room furnished in greens and reds.

The frame of a picture should be given careful consideration. One point never to forget is that an ornate frame does not add to a picture but detracts from it. The purpose of a frame is to enclose, to separate the picture from the wall, to guide the eyes into the picture, to help center attention on it. The purpose of a frame is not to adorn a picture but to give it exclusive, concentrated entity.

White walls, as we know, are an optical strain and a psychological hazard. Small spots of white, however, are very effective. White or near-white frames reflect light into the picture and provide an excellent contrasting border against a richly colored or deep-toned wall. For water colors (originals or prints), a white mat with a narrow frame of natural wood is generally effective because the natural wood provides an optical stepping stone between the white mat and deep-colored wall.

A typical home nowadays may contain about a dozen pictures and little or no art of any other kind. The typical home of the future will probably have a better balance—perhaps six pictures and six pieces of sculpture. Ceramics, too, will be more in evidence.

One reason for this change is that an increasing number of modern dwellings are being built with picture windows, glass walls and partitions and built-in shelves and cases. Such homes have less space for hanging pictures and more accommodations for three-dimensional art. In a home of this type, an ideal background is provided for sculpture and ceramics.

As in the case of pictures, original pieces of sculpture will be available only to those who can afford them. Most people will have reproductions. Since sculpture is easily and inexpensively reproduced in plastics or plaster, we may expect a rapid growth in the popularity of this art.

Ceramics are not costly now. A brisk demand will bring the cost down still more. There is no reason why the most modest home cannot have beautifully and richly colored ceramics as accents in every room.

If you have examined the illustrations in this book, you have noted a view of the gallery wall in the living room of the Cheskin home. Three paintings (of my own) are on the long living room wall and fifteen original pieces of sculpture on the mantle and bookcases which occupy the length of the wall. In the study there is a similar arrangement, with the gallery wall having three pictures and the bookcase supporting nine original pieces of sculpture. Each corner in the living room has a large piece of sculpture. We have small sculptured works and my own drawings and paintings in all the other rooms, including the bedrooms.

The sculpture gives a variety of interest to the rooms. Ten sculptors are represented. Each style is unique, interesting, inspiring to emotions and mind. Furniture must by its nature have predominantly horizontal and perpendicular lines which tend to monotony. The sculptured pieces are not limited by physical function. They are diverse in shape and proportion. Some are realistic, some stylized, some abstract. Some have rough texture, and some are polished. All of them combined give a variety of interest and stimulation to us and to most of our guests.

I have suggested that you try painting your own pictures. But you may be more sensitive to form than to color, and clay modeling may appeal to you more than painting. It may be easier for you to master a three-dimensional medium than a two-dimensional one. If you don't know, try them both. You will soon find out.

Whether you buy pictures and pieces of sculpture or produce them yourself—whether you can afford original works of art or reproductions, keep in mind that pictures and three-dimensional forms are essential for the home. Works of art are humanizing elements. They incorporate in miniature the universal elements of diversity, movement, harmony and unity; they convey the creative impulse and character of the artist. A work of art in your home means that part of the artist lives with you and enriches your home and your life.

9. Color In The Home of The Future

It is noteworthy that art and architecture lost their natural functions, even for many of the wealthy, in the early days of the Industrial Revolution. While some people of means clung to the aesthetic patterns of their fathers, others began to gratify their personal whims chiefly by aping various elements of ancient or exotic cultures.

In a constantly widening area, color became almost meaningless except as it was associated with rare stones, precious metals and intricately designed objects of past centuries. Ostentatious residences were built with Ionic or Corinthian columns, with Gothic or Renaissance arches, with elaborately carved cornices. Even the Oriental cultures were drawn upon for ideas that could be introduced into the home to make it look "different" and to display the wealth of the owner.

As for the dwellings of the poor, these became nothing but rows of shacks in factory districts, not really fit for human habitation. In these blighted areas, color largely ceased to be. Smoke and grime and coal dust obliterated hues and tints.

After nearly two centuries of this period of false aestheticism—a hodgepodge, as far as the well-to-do were concerned, of feudal hang-overs, exotic importations and personal caprice—a number of major developments took place.

Economic conditions gradually improved for industrial workers. New machines were invented that required increased operating skills with a corresponding rise in wages. Fast transportation and other decentralizing factors made it possible for factory personnel to live at considerable distances from their places of employment. With the constantly rising standard of living, slums began to disappear and beauty gained a chance to enter (or re-enter) the average man's life.

Today we look forward to the total elimination of both poverty-stricken districts of shanties and useless, cluttered, ostentatious mansions. Goods of quality and in quantity will be turned out by the machine in ever-increasing abundance for all. We may expect that functional design, with its integration of beauty and utility, will shape more and more of our material environment. The power of color will become better understood, and with this growing color-consciousness will come a deepening of human satisfactions.

Specifically, art and color in the home of the future, if they are to meet the social and psychological needs of people living in an atomic age, will follow a fairly predictable evolutionary course. Architecture and furnishings will become increasingly functional. The use of color within the home will become more flexible and effective.

Colored lights may be incorporated into interior design.

In that case, the home owner, by pressing a button, will be able to produce a warmly colored wall when he needs stimulation and a cool wall when he desires a restful background.

The restorative and therapeutic effects of color, already studied and utilized by psychologists, will find suitable domestic application. Industry will color-tune its products, and articles for the home will be available in appropriate hues, shades, tints and tones. All these and many other similar developments are already forerunners of the "shape of things to come."

In short, the science of color, particularly in its psychological aspects, will undergo expansion. We have already made a brave beginning. In the years ahead, the home will become, much more than it is now, a planned unit for living, glowing and vibrant, individualistic yet also a harmonious part of an integrated community. Its beauties of color will seem as fundamental in the scheme of things as air and food. Then, perhaps, we will have taken a long step forward in the art of living.

CHAPTER FOUR

The Four Sides of Color: Physical, Chemical, Physiological and Psychological

1. Physical Aspects of Color

This chapter, which is in part a summary of what has gone before, is a discussion of the basic nature of color in nontechnical language. It is planned to provide you with handy reference material, for you are probably a person who takes an intelligent interest in all sides of an important subject, even though knowledge of many of the facts contained herein is not absolutely essential for the effective color-tuning of your home. At any rate, knowing the whys and wherefores of color can be helpful on a practical level in increasing the efficiency of what you are doing.

Let us begin by considering the relationship between light and color. As you probably remember from your school days, the colors we see when a ray of light is passed through a prism are commonly called violet, blue, green, yellow, orange and red. Each color in this sequence, called the spectrum, corresponds to a specific wave length.

When Isaac Newton, the famous physicist, first broke up a ray of light with a prism in 1666, he named a seventh color —indigo. However, although indigo and many other colors can be seen in a laboratory, only the six from violet to red are evident to the naked eye.

Different sources of light have different percentages of spectral color distribution. A ray of ordinary daylight contains very little violet. The other colors are present in about equal proportion, though there is just a little less red and a little more blue than any of the other hues. The time of day is a factor in the proportioning of the colors.

A ray of direct sunlight has very little violet. It has a little less blue than ordinary daylight, and in comparison with north light, has much less blue, less green, just a little more yellow and much more orange and red.

North light has more violet than ordinary daylight, much more blue, a little more green, less yellow, much less orange and still less red.

A daylight fluorescent tube has the spectral colors in about the same proportion as natural daylight.

An incandescent electric bulb or a white fluorescent tube has a maximum of red, a large amount of orange and yellow, very little green, a mere touch of blue and hardly any violet.

This type of light is commonly known as yellow or warm light.

The uneven distribution of spectral colors shows why some light is cold and some warm. Light containing a maximum of red, orange and yellow with red predominant is warm. Light containing a maximum of violet, blue and green (least of green) is cold.

It is worth noting that the hues which make white light either cool or warm are the hues classified as cool or warm in pigments. Here we see a direct relationship of light to surface colors. Needless to say, the terms "cold" and "warm," as used in relation to light and pigments, do not refer to sensations of temperature but to visual and psychological experiences.

The color of an object depends on two factors: the light in which the object is seen and its pigmentation. Cold light makes an object cooler-looking no matter what its "actual" color is, and warm light makes it appear warmer. Thus the type of lighting has a great effect on all surface colors.

You can readily understand how light affects surface color by considering that a white sheet of paper in a room filled with blue light would not look white but blue. A more dramatic example of the interaction between light and surface color is seen in the fact that when a green light is turned on a red object, the surface of the object will appear black.

The belief in one or the other of two half-truths—one that color is light, the other that color is pigment—is responsible for many of the difficulties and perplexities that beset workers in color. The fact is, of course, that color "resides" in both light and substance; it is a manifestation of the relationship between the two.

The significant point for our consideration here, however,

is that the three primaries of light are different from the three primaries of pigment. The primary colors of light are red, blue and green—or more exactly, orange-red, violet-blue and green. All others are derived from these by additive mixtures. We must not be confused at this point by the fact that to artists, designers and printers the primaries are red, blue and yellow—to be more precise—magenta red, green-blue and yellow. The first set of primaries deals with light, the second with pigments. Let us explore this subject a bit further.

There is a direct relationship between the primaries of light and the primaries of pigment. This can be best understood by considering that each pigment primary reflects exactly two-thirds of white light and absorbs the other third. The absorbed third is the complementary color. Examples of this relationship are given below.

Since each pigment primary absorbs one-third of white light (or one primary of light), a mixture of two pigment primaries which forms a secondary color, absorbs two-thirds of white light (or two primaries of light).

This means that while a primary pigment, as we have noted, reflects two-thirds of light (two light primaries), a secondary pigment reflects one-third of light (one light primary).

Combining two primary colors of *light* produces one primary color of *pigment;* conversely, combining two primaries of *pigment* yields one primary of *light*. In other words, a secondary color of pigment corresponds to a primary color of light, and a secondary color of light results in a primary color of pigment.

A primary color of pigment and a primary color of light (which is a secondary color of pigment) are complementary because together they reflect the full gamut of colors, which is white.

Absorbed hues are thus the exact complementaries to reflected hues. You see orange-red because the green-blue has been absorbed by the pigment in the object, and you see green-blue because the orange-red has been absorbed. In a similar way, green is white light minus magenta red, and magenta red is white light minus green. Violet-blue is white light minus yellow, and yellow is white light minus violet-blue.

All substances subtract light, that is, they absorb parts of it and reflect the rest. Hence nature presents a diversity of colors such as grays, browns, greens, reds and blues. The degree, or selectivity, of absorption and reflection of light depends on the chemical nature of the substance. The chemical nature of a white object is such that it reflects nearly all of the light that strikes it. Most whites are not pure and absorb from 3 to 10 per cent of light.

Complementary hues are any two hues, which together are composed of equal amounts of all three primaries, either of pigment or light.

For producing exact complementaries and for practical use in mixing and matching pigment colors, we must have three primary pigments, each of which absorbs one-third or one primary of light. Green-blue absorbs orange-red, magenta red absorbs green and yellow absorbs violet-blue.

In producing shades, black pigment is used. Black is not a fourth color (except psychologically) but the sum of the three primaries in relation to light. A pigment primary subtracts or absorbs one-third of light, and a secondary pigment (a mixture of two primaries) absorbs two-thirds of light. Thus, the three primaries combined absorb all the light. In other words, mixing equal amounts of the three *primary pigments* results in black because the combination cuts off all light reflection.

However, although complementary-colored lights produce white light, mixing equal quantities of *complementary pigments* will not produce black because of the quantitative element of primary color content. If one mixes, for example, an ounce (bulk or weight) of magenta red with an ounce of green, the mixture is actually one ounce of magenta red with the combination making up the green—a half ounce of yellow and a half ounce of green-blue. To produce black there must be two ounces of green with one ounce of magenta red because the three primaries must be equal in quantity as well as in strength.

This further means that a hue consisting, for example, of thirteen parts yellow and three parts blue would involve a complicated measuring problem in order to produce black (or a gray by including white) by mixing this hue with its complementary. Therefore, in mixing shades and tones of paints, it is advisable to use black pigment, which automatically is the sum of the three primaries in subtracting light.

Converting a hue into a shade by adding black actually means subtracting some of the brilliance or purity from the substance with black. Producing a tint, by adding white pigment, means adding white light to the hue. Producing a tone by adding black and white means subtracting some of the brilliance from the hue and at the same time adding white light.

Because pigment colors subtract light, mixing or adding pigment colors is called a subtractive process. And the paint or printing-ink primaries—green-blue, magenta red and yellow—are, scientifically speaking, subtractive primaries. Mixing colored lights is called an additive process, and orange-red, green and violet-blue are termed additive primaries.

The subtractive process with pigment primaries is used

in half-tone color printing, but the solid colors seen by the eye result from the additive mixture of the color dots of the screen. In other words, the eye cannot see the tiny individual dots but "mixes" into a single color the host of colored lights which the dots reflect. Half-tone color printing is, therefore, a combination of subtractive and additive color mixing.

This brief discussion of the physical side of color would hardly serve its purpose without some reference to the importance of light and color in science and industry. For example, certain colorless materials admit ultra-violet radiations; color is used to keep such radiation out where it would be injurious. For years glass containers have been colored brown or dark green to protect drugs and foods from harmful rays. Thus color plays a physical role in the preservation of health.

2. Chemical Aspects of Color

While physicists can split a ray of light into three parts and thus establish three primary hues of specific wave lengths, chemists on the other hand, have not produced three substances that can be used systematically for mixing all pigment colors. Blue is produced with cobalt, ultramarine and phthalocyanine. Which of these is the primary, basic pigment? Which is a primary yellow, cadmium or chrome? And of the dozens of reds, which is the primary?

Moreover, there are variations of hue and of value even in the same chemical. Phthalocyanine or cobalt blue, for example, can be purplish or greenish, light or deep. Putting it another way, blue can be produced from a number of chemicals, each having a different wave length. The same is true of yellow and red.

A number of problems are posed in formulating three

balanced, accurate and constant primaries. First of all, the latter must be exact in hue so that they will correspond to secondary colors of light. Secondly, pigments have different specific gravities, and have to be balanced in strength on a bulk or weight basis so that they can be used in a system for color mixing. Thirdly, primaries should be colors that will not fade. Production controls are necessary to maintain these primary color characteristics.

Still another point in color chemistry is that pigments cannot be mixed properly unless they have a chemical affinity for one another. Lake compounds cannot be mixed with lead, copper or earth colors. A lake color is a compound of organic pigment on an inorganic base. Alizarin crimson is a lake color, a coal-tar derivative. Cadmium yellow is derived from cadmium sulphide. Chrome yellow is a lead chromate. Cobalt blue is a metallic element. Cerulean blue is a form of cobalt. Vermilion is made of mercury and sulphur. Titanium white is a metallic element.

Because of the impurities of pigments and because of the desire for maximum brilliance, six basic hues—two blues (cerulean and ultramarine), two reds (alizarin and vermilion) and two yellows (lemon and chrome)—are sometimes used for mixing.

The very brightest hues can be obtained by using cerulean (or cyan) blue for mixing with lemon yellow to make greens, ultramarine blue (or cobalt) for mixing with alizarin (rose madder or rhodamine) to make violet and vermilion for mixing with chrome (or cadmium) to produce the brightest possible orange colors.

But getting a set of three basic colors for mixing constitutes enough of a problem in production control. Six basic colors mean twice as many problems. Striving for the brightest possible hues is like chasing the rainbow (which is beautiful while it lasts), but who needs a permanent rainbow in the house? For all practical purposes, three pigment primaries will give you all the hues in as pure and vibrant a state as you will ever want.

The color charts in this book show twelve hues, one on each chart, produced from a set of three primaries. They are much too brilliant for any large area in your home. You may want one or a pair of the pure hues in a picture, draperies, upholstery or a ceramic piece, but not on the walls or rug.

When you buy anything in a bright color, get assurance that it will not fade. Always remember that although pigment color depends on light, it is chemical in nature, and that a color, like love, may be either permanent or fleeting.

3. Physiological Aspects of Color

According to physiologists and psychologists there are four primary hues—red, green, blue and yellow. Offhand, this looks like a compromise between the primaries of the physicist and those of the artist. Actually, physiological primaries are determined by a study of the anatomy and physiology of the human eye.

Colors produce sensations and therefore come under the province of physiology. Psychologically speaking, the study of sensations cannot be systematized like mathematics because sensory perception is partly subjective, but the physical factors that enter into sensations can be measured and formulated into an objective scheme.

The theory of color vision is highly complex, and we have still much to learn about it. Among the most interesting facts is the way in which color blindness manifests itself, either in relation to red and green or to blue and yellow. A person who is totally color-blind perceives colors only as different values, or varying intensities, of gray. (Perhaps you did not know that dogs and cats do not see color but that birds and fish do.)

Because physiologists find color blindness in complementary pairs, they have reason to conclude that red and green are perceived through one set of receptors in the eye and blue and yellow through another set. Of course, this is not strange, in view of the fact that sets of complementary colors make up the whole of the visible spectrum. Magenta red, for example, is one part of white light, and green is the other part. The perception of color in complementary pairs is a natural occurrence.

The phenomenon of the after-image also demonstrates the link between the physiological and the physical aspects of color and light. The after-image of red is green; the after-image of blue is yellow—and vice versa.

The human eye is anatomically and physiologically equipped to receive the entire visible spectrum (white light) as well as its component parts (colors). When the eye becomes saturated with a color, which is a portion of the visible spectrum, and then is directed to a white surface, which reflects the full gamut of visible energy, that part of energy or light that has not saturated the eye appears on the white surface in the form of a complementary color. We need not enlarge upon this subject here, since the after-image was amply discussed in the first chapter.

Simultaneous contrast, the phenomenon of a color appearing lighter next to a very deep color and darker next to a very light color, is not a physical but a psychological effect. It is akin to the apparently diminished size of an object next to a much larger one and the apparently increased size of the first object next to a much smaller one. The cause of this effect is often confused with that of the after-image, which rests upon an entirely different basis—a physical one.

It should be borne in mind that problems of exact definition concerning the "physical" and the "physiological," the "objective" and the "subjective," have preoccupied scientists and philosophers for ages, and it is not the purpose of this book to do anything but discuss each sphere of color in the broadest possible terms.

4. Psychological Aspects of Color

The spectrum is physical; the materials out of which we prepare pigments are chemical; the perception of color is physiological, as well as physical. The major importance of colors to us, however, is in their psychological effects.

Light and color have always played a prominent role in human affairs. The primitive peoples of Asia and the ancient Greeks associated colors with the sun and with divinity. These people represented life and goodness by bright colors, death and evil by black. They used brilliant colors almost everywhere and identified them with godliness.

In our day we are immersed in the same world of color but have gained a more systematized knowledge about it. Accordingly we are in a better position to use color for specific objectives.

Though we occasionally hear people express strong likes and dislikes for different colors, the impact of color sensations is usually upon the unconscious. People are not often aware that colors have a tremendous influence on them. They seldom realize that a person may be unconscious of the colors around him and yet be powerfully affected by them with regard to mood, temperament and behavior.

We should not forget that color sensations sometimes

produce physical reactions. People often feel cold in a blue room and warm in a red room without realizing that colors, not physical temperature, are responsible for the difference in effects.

Colors are divided into two distinct psychological groups —cool and warm. The cool colors are blue or predominantly blue in cast. The warm colors are red or any predominantly red and yellow. Complementary colors are warm-cool pairs.

Significant in its bearing on human well-being is the fact that cool colors have a sedative effect and have proved calming to highly nervous people who feel uncomfortable in an environment of warm colors. Less excitable people become depressed in surroundings of strong blue and have their spirits lifted by reds and yellows. There is a strong tendency for most persons to seek unconsciously a balanced diet of calming and stimulating colors by surrounding themselves with tints and tones derived from both cool and warm hues.

Of greatest value is the knowledge that colors should be used in complementary pairs, because the relationship between complementary colors is physical, physiological and psychological. Complementary hues comprise the total visible spectrum, are physiological pairs in the eyes and provide a psychological balance of warmth and coolness. In other words complementary colors are physically, optically and psychologically balanced.

It is worth remembering that the easiest way to understand the nature of color is to recognize that every hue has a mate and a family. The complementary hue is the mate, and the related values—shades, tints and tones—are the family.

According to traditional aesthetic concepts, use of complementary colors is in good taste. Actually, acquired taste has little to do with this preference, since, for physical and optical reasons, it is as natural for normal people to like complementary colors as it is for them to walk upright. Where complementary color combinations are not preferred there is likely to be some kind of special conditioning or an adverse economic factor. This is indicated by the fact that many primitive peoples create designs in complementary colors, whereas discordant color conglomerations are often found in industrial slums.

Preference tests made by an indirect method at Color Research Institute for the purpose of probing unconscious levels suggest that colors normally affect people in accordance with specific laws. Some colors have high preference ratings, others extremely low ones. It was found that some colors rate higher with men than with women and vice versa (men usually preferring deep shades while women like delicate tints), and that some hues get progressively higher or lower preference ratings as they are diluted or neutralized with increasing amounts of white or gray. Color preference can hardly be a purely subjective matter when there is such correlation between degrees of color preference and degrees of hue modification.

While neutral colors call forth no strong emotional responses in either men or women, primary hues produce clear-cut reactions. Apparently a person either likes a pure hue or he doesn't; there is no gradation of feeling for pure hues as with shades, tints and tones. For example, if he likes pure blue, he will not express a stronger or weaker liking for pure green; green, too, will be either liked or disliked. That same person, however, will have degrees of preference for dark blue, light blue and very light blue, although liking them all.

The preference rating of a color is conditioned not only by its specific tonal value but also by the presence of other colors, by the area it occupies and by the object with which it is associated.

When a color is used with its complementary, the preference rating usually rises. Thus, green has increased appeal when it is used near magenta red and orange-red becomes more acceptable in the company of green-blue. Presumably, of course, this is due to the physical and optical relationship between complementary colors. However, a pure red which may be pleasing against a neutral background sometimes is found much too vibrant when associated with its complementary green, particularly if the green is not sufficiently diluted or neutralized. The same is true about other complementaries.

Dosage, or the quantitative element, is as important in color as it is in everything else. The powerful effect of a hue can be cut down, by limiting the area which it covers, just as well as by diluting it with white or neutralizing it with gray. A mildly stimulating effect can be created in a room by covering the walls with peach, which is produced by diluting orange-red, or by having orange-red objects or accessories in a room with a neutral background.

Associations, or symbolic elements, strongly affect color preference ratings. For example, magenta red, which has a high general preference rating, drops in rating when it is put into the kitchen. Orange-red, which has one of the lowest general preference ratings, increases in preference when used in the kitchen on walls or in utensils or stool covers. Colors of the peach-pink group receive increased preference ratings when associated with cosmetics and drop in preference when linked with hardware.

A large percentage of people shows preference for a certain green when that color is associated with a vacation. The same green drops in preference when it is used with various food products. Another green has a high rating when associated with food but a low rating when associated with clothing. Still another green has a high rate of acceptance when seen with jewelry but falls in preference rating when associated with cosmetics.

Rarity is also a factor in color preference. Colors seen only occasionally possess the emotionally stimulating elements of surprise and newness. Common colors, like common foods, are monotonous; they may become tiresome and prompt us to look for new color sensations.

Another fact about color preference is that it does not necessarily coincide with color retention. Yellow, for instance, has a low preference rating but a high retention rating. In other words, although yellow is not well liked it is easily recalled. Peach, on the other hand, while a favorite with most people, is difficult to remember. Some colors, however, have the same ratings for preference and for retention.

Tests conducted at Color Research Institute on the basis of what people want (not what they say they like) also reveal that there are geographic, national, cultural and economic factors in color preference. For example, a specific red received a much higher preference rating with Italians and Mexicans than with Scandinavians and New Englanders. And it had a much higher preference rating with Italians in low-income groups than with upper middle-income Italians. A cool magenta red had a very high general preference rating but a much lower one among the underprivileged. A grass-green color had a low preference rating in rural communities and a very high rating in a steel mill community.

Higher education and higher income coincided with preference for delicate colors. Illiteracy and poverty coincided with preference for brilliant colors.

For practical purposes, research showed that persons who had many emotional outlets through culture and/or ability to purchase emotional satisfaction showed a preference for diluted and neutralized colors. Those who had opportunity for only limited emotional outlets (either because of lack of education or because of low income) showed a distinct preference for pure hues in large doses, particularly for those that were warm, such as orange-red and red-orange. For the underprivileged, the nearer the colors are to those of the rainbow the more enticing they are.

Generally speaking, magenta red and blue are very popular colors, but yellow-green has a low preference rating. Blue-green has much higher preference than yellow-green. Although popular as a pure hue, magenta red becomes generally unacceptable when diluted with white. A pure orange-red has a very low preference rating, but when mixed with white, and thus converted into peach, its preference rating is high.

There is reason to believe, on the basis of psychoanalytical studies, that persons who show strongly abnormal color preferences also possess other abnormal characteristics and that abnormal reactions to certain colors can often be traced to unfortunate experiences in formative years.

Women who show a preference for colors normally preferred by men exhibit other masculine characteristics. Men who prefer delicate or "feminine" tints show other effeminate traits. Individuals who shun any suggestion of a pure hue are often found to be overly inhibited persons who fear to express themselves emotionally.

Individuals who have an aversion to red or blue may find their negative feelings traceable to a painful childhood experience in connection with those colors. However, these people generally are not aware of the connection between their color phobias or obsessions and early traumatic experiences.

In conclusion: color is an optical and psychological factor everywhere. Colors affect our emotions at work and at play. Some colors create a pleasant mood; others produce discord and irritability. Emotional stability and efficiency depend to a great extent on environment, of which color is a most important element. By learning the nature of color we can harness its power and use it for our emotional well-being and general welfare.

CHAPTER FIVE

Tools for Color Planning

1. How to Use the Color Charts

Now I am going to show you how to use the color charts for arranging a harmonious color scheme for your room.

Turn to chart number 1. You see that the upper left hand rectangle is a brilliant yellow (hue). As you look down the column of colors directly underneath, you see that each yellow is lighter than the one above it. These progressively lighter yellows are made by adding more and more white to the bright yellow. They are "tints" of yellow. (A tint is a pure hue plus white.) The tints are marked *a, b, c* and *d*. Tint *d* has the most white added.

Now return to the pure yellow hue in the upper left hand corner. Instead of glancing downward, glance straight across to the right. You see that each color (on that page) is progressively darker than the one to its left. These darker yellows are made by adding more and more black to the bright yellow hue. They are "shades" of yellow. (A shade is a pure hue plus black.) The shades are numbered *1, 2, 3* and *4*.

All of the colors which are not directly in the column under the hue or directly in the top row across from it contain yellow plus both white and black. They are called "tones" of yellow. (A tone is a hue plus both white and black.)

The color in the column under *4* in the *a* row has, of all colors shown on the page, the most black and the least white added to the yellow. We call this color *1-a-4*. (It is on chart 1, in row *a* and in column *4*. The color in column *1* and in row *d* (called *1-d-1*) has the most white and the least black. The color in column *4* and in row *d* (called *1-d-4*) has the most of both white and black. All the colors on this chart are related because they are made from one hue—yellow.

You know after looking over the number 1 chart that a middle tone of yellow such as *1-b-2* is yellow with white and black. But you may call it by another name, perhaps olive. Names do not describe colors accurately. That is why we use numbers and letters for designating colors.

Now look at the opposite chart, number 7. The hue in the upper left hand corner is violet-blue. Once again, the colors in the top row are shades of violet-blue, the colors directly beneath the pure hue are tints of violet-blue and the others are tones of violet-blue. All of the colors (except the pure hue) on the page are made by adding white, black or both to the brilliant hue (pure color) in the upper left corner. All the colors on chart **7** are related because they are all made from violet-blue.

Charts 1 and 7 are placed opposite each other for a reason: they are complementary sets of colors. Yellow and violet-blue together form a "whole" to the eye. Complementary colors are physically, optically and psychologically balanced. That's why all of the colors on a pair of facing charts are normally pleasing.

Any color or colors on chart 1 can be combined in a color plan with any other color or colors on either chart 1 or chart 7 to make an effective color scheme.

You can see that limiting color combinations to two basic hues does not mean restricting yourself to using a limited number of colors. Many values of each of the two hues can be combined to produce harmonious effects. You can have a combination of as many as four or five values of magenta red with an equal or lesser number of toned, tinted or shaded greens. Numerous color combinations are possible by using various values of complementary hues. White or gray and even black in small areas can always be part of a color plan.

In planning color for a room, you must first determine the dominant color, which is generally to be on your walls, on the floor or in large upholstered furniture. Find this color on a chart, and you automatically have before your eyes fifty related and complementary colors from which to choose.

Which specific colors you choose to use with the dominant color depends on personal preference, lighting conditions and the availability of the materials or objects in the shades, tones and tints you prefer.

You may be familiar with color circles or color wheels. The color wheel is an extension in circular form of the spectral band of hues. Some circles consist of six spectral hues only; some extend the hues to twelve and others to twenty-four. The additional hues are obtained, of course, by mixing the primaries.

Complementary hues are always opposite each other on the color circle, and if the three primary colors in the circle are connected by lines, a triangle is formed. Any three hues on the circle forming an equilateral triangle are known as a triad.

You probably are familiar with split complementary color harmonies. Splitting a color means substituting for it any two colors that are equidistant from it on the color circle.

Split color harmonies have for years been advocated by artists and designers, but they are not recommended here because they are psychologically negative.

Since we respond favorably to a physical, optical and psychological pair of hues (complementaries) a third hue is, to say the least, superfluous. Combinations of more than two pure hues, in a permanent situation such as in your home, are not only gaudy but also taxing to the emotions.

You probably have heard about analogous colors. Analogous colors resemble each other because they are in the same quarter of the circle. In a twelve-color circle yellow-green, yellow and orange are analogous. This is a combination of three warm vibrant colors. Analogous colors violet, violet-blue and blue are a set of three cold colors. In either combination, you have a lack of physical, optical and psychological balance.

Even in using color combinations based on two complementary hues, keep in mind that one of the hues should predominate; the second one should be diluted or neutralized in varying degrees or used as small accents. Always remember that limiting color combinations to two hues does not mean an undue restriction in the number of colors but only in the number of basic hues.

Noncomplementary colors in your room will not interfere with eye-ease if they are neutral in tone, such as gray, beige, tan or the color of wood. You should not, however, have large objects and/or expanses of rich colors that are not complementary, such as a blue sofa in a green and magenta red room.

For large areas such as walls, rug and furniture coverings, you should choose colors only from facing complementary charts if you wish to obtain pleasing effects.

It is not necessary to match a color exactly in tonal value. Make sure that you have complementary colors but feel free, as far as color harmony is concerned, to choose from any of the fifty colors on a pair of charts.

When matching drapery or upholstery fabric, if you are not sure whether you have the right color, check the charts immediately following and preceding to determine whether these charts have a closer match to your sample. For instance, if you think chart 5 has your color, check with chart 4 and chart 6 to be sure you are right.

Tweeds or broken-color materials should be placed about four or five feet away for matching because small spots of color mix in the eye at a distance.

2. Mixing the Colors in Paint

The 9 secondary hues and 288 tints, tones and shades shown on the charts can be produced from magenta red, green-blue, yellow, black and white.

The three primary pigment hues, Yellow No. 1, Magenta Red No. 5 and Green-Blue No. 9 can be obtained in most paint stores. You should have this book with you when you go to purchase the primary colors. Show the primary colors to the store clerk so that he can help you get the right colors for mixing.

From the three primaries—yellow, magenta red and green-blue—follow the procedures given below for obtaining the nine secondary hues.

HUE NUMBER

1 (Yellow)	Cannot be mixed—get from store
2 (Orange)	Mix two parts yellow with one part magenta red
3 (Orange-Red)	Mix one part yellow with one part magenta red
4 (Red)	Mix one part yellow with two parts magenta red
5 (Magenta red)	Cannot be mixed—get from store
6 (Violet)	Mix two parts magenta red with one part green-blue
7 (Violet-Blue)	Mix one part magenta red with one part green-blue
8 (Blue)	Mix one part magenta red with two parts green-blue
9 (Green-Blue)	Cannot be mixed—get from store
10 (Blue-Green)	Mix two parts green-blue with one part yellow
11 (Green)	Mix one part green-blue with one part yellow
12 (Yellow-Green)	Mix one part green-blue with two parts yellow

If the primary colors are balanced in tinting strength the exact proportions given above will produce the desired color. If your primary paints are not perfectly balanced in tinting strength, which is quite likely, the given proportions are approximate. Therefore, when mixing a hue from two primaries you may have to use a bit more or a bit less of one of the primaries.

Even with unbalanced primaries, for mixing any hue, you have only one unknown factor. For example, in mixing green, you need a little more or less either of the yellow or of the green-blue (turquoise). For mixing a violet-blue you need a little more or less either of the green-blue (turquoise) or the magenta red. For mixing an orange, you need a little more or less either of the magenta red or the yellow.

To mix a shade add black to the pure hue. The amount of black depends on the strength of the pigment. Add the black a little at a time because it is very potent. You can always add more black if you find it necessary to get a more accurate match. If you begin by adding too much black, you will have to add more of the pure hue, which may cause you to mix more paint than you need.

You can produce black by mixing the three primary pigments. A black can also be made by mixing ultramarine or cobalt blue with sienna or umber. Three balanced primaries make the richest black. However, black paint is cheap; the primary colors are expensive.

To mix a tint add white to the pure hue. In discussing the mixing of most tints, it is more appropriate to speak of adding the pure hue to the white, because so much more white has to be used. For very deep tints you generally need one part of pure hue to three parts of white. A tint of medium depth requires, as a rule, one part of pure hue added to six, seven or eight parts of white. A light tint can be mixed with one part of pure hue and sixteen parts of white. The exact amount depends on the purity and strength of the hue.

If you find that your tint is too raw (more brilliant than the color on the printed chart) add a small amount of the complementary hue. A touch of green will gray a peach. A small amount of red will gray a green tint.

To mix a tone you must first produce a tint. Then you add black to the tint to get a tone. In other words, first match the hue, then mix the hue with white to match the tint and finally add a small quantity of black to match the tone.

For example, to mix the blue-green tone **10-*b*-1,** first make pure hue No. **10** by mixing two parts green-blue with one part yellow. Then mix with white until you get a satisfactory match to **10-*b*.** Finally add a touch of black to get the blue-green tone **10-*b*-1.**

With this procedure of producing a tone there is only one unknown factor at each step in the process of arriving at the desired tone.

Interior I. The Author's Living Room.   *Courtesy of Rochelle's Furniture Co.*   *Photo by Krantzen*
This color plan is based on Complementary Color Charts No. 4 and No. 10. Fireplace, rug and drapery are derived from red; walls and upholstered furniture are tones of the complementary blue-green.

Interior II. The Author's Kitchen. *Courtesy of Consoweld Corp.* *Photo by Krantzen*

This color plan is based on Complementary Color Charts No. 4 and No. 10. The warm tones of counters and floor are balanced with the complementary tone of blue-green on the walls.

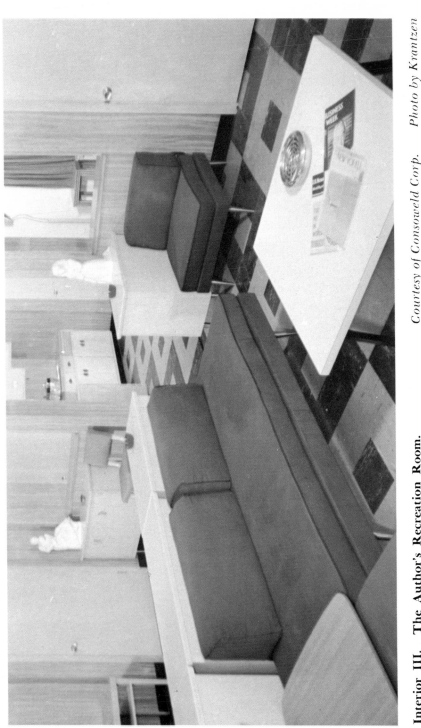

Interior III. The Author's Recreation Room. *Courtesy of Consoweld Corp.* *Photo by Krantzen*

This color plan is based on Complementary Color Charts No. 3 and No. 9. The light and deep tones of the floor derived from orange-red, are complemented with a deep shade of green-blue.

Interior IV.

Courtesy of B. Stromberg Construction Co.   Photo by Krantzen

This color plan is based on Complementary Color Charts No. 2 and No. 8.   The warm colors dominate.

Interior V.

This color plan is based on Complementary Color Charts No. 2 and No. 8. Light, middle and deep tones derived from orange are complemented with tones of blue.

Interior VI.

Courtesy of B. Stromberg Construction Co.   Photo by Krantzen

This color plan is based on Complementary Color Charts No. 6 and No. 12. The neutral tones of the floor derived from violet are accented with light complementary tones derived from chartreuse.

Interior VII.   *Courtesy of The Howell Co.   Photo by Chesterfield*

This color plan is based on Complementary Color Charts No. 3 and No. 9. The warm-tone rug is complemented with muted green-blue furniture.

Interior VIII.

Courtesy of Kroehler Mfg. Co.   *Photo by Hedrich-Blessing*

This color plan is based on Complementary Color Charts No. 1 and No. 7. Light and middle tones of violet-blue are combined with light complementary tones of yellow.

Interior IX.   *Courtesy of B. Stromberg Construction Co.   Photo by Krantzen*

This color plan is based on Complementary Color Charts No. 3 and No. 9. Predominantly warm tones are accented with green-blue.

Interior X.

Courtesy of Consoweld Corp.   *Photo by R. F. Hildebrand*

This color plan is based on Complementary Color Charts No. 3 and No. 9. Light and middle tones derived from orange-red are complemented with green-blue.

Interior XI.

Courtesy of McCoy-Couch Furniture Mfg. Co.   Photo by Leonard

This color plan is based on Complementary Color Charts No. 5 and No. 11.   The green tones of the walls and rug

Interior XII.

Courtesy of Kroehler Mfg. Co.   *Photo by Hedrich-Blessing*

This color plan is based on Complementary Color Charts No. 4 and No. 10. Light and middle tones of blue-green are complemented with middle tones derived from red.

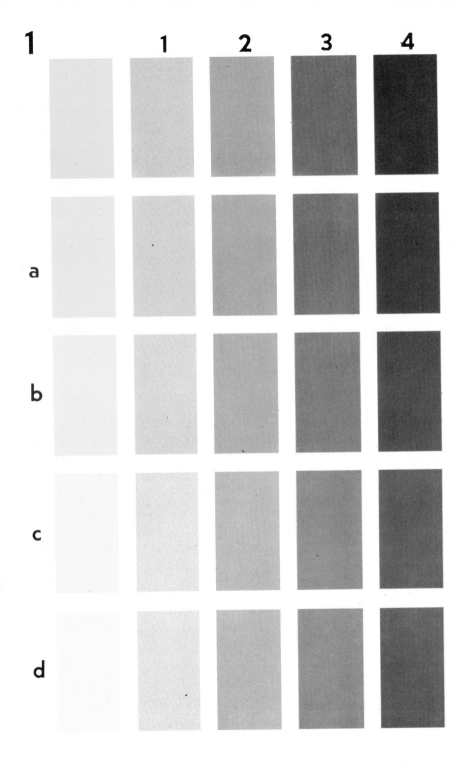

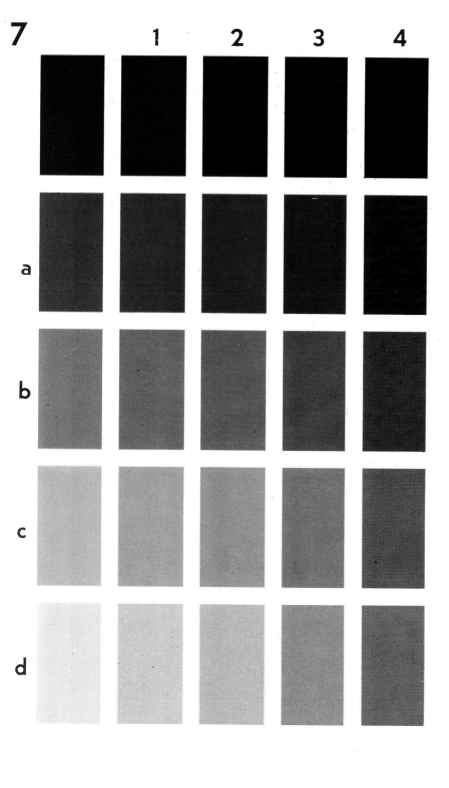

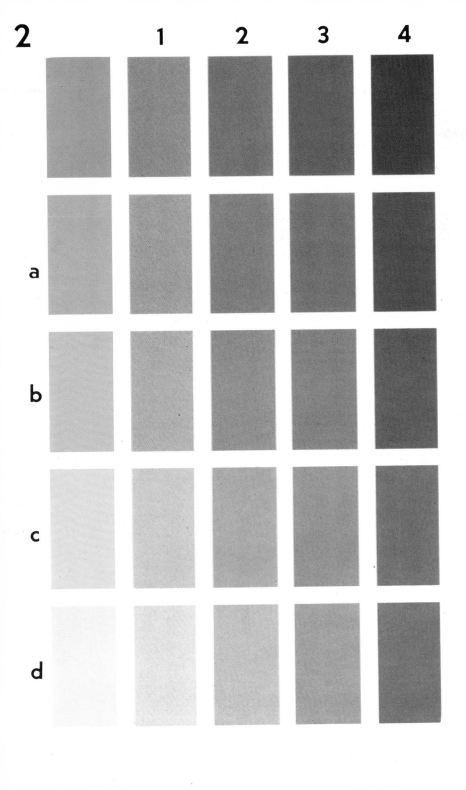

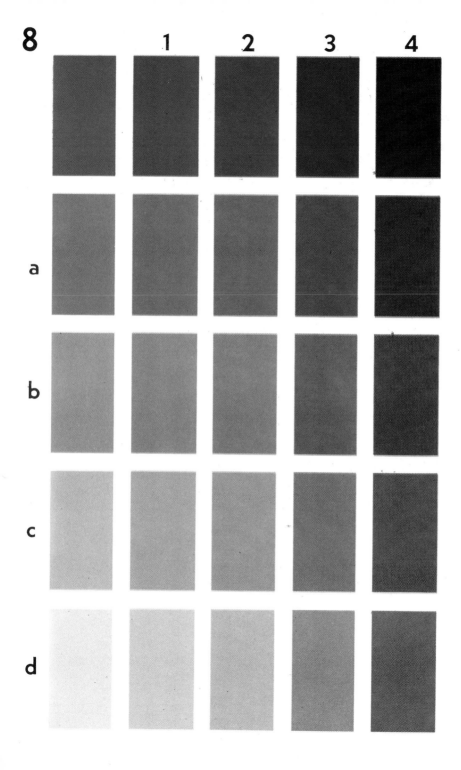

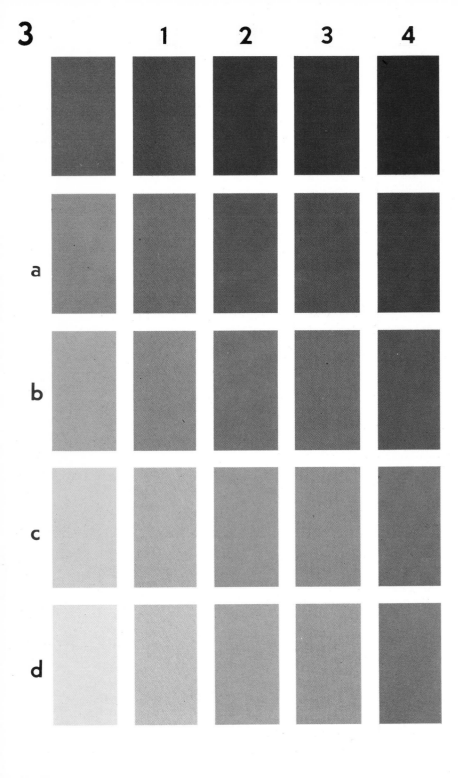

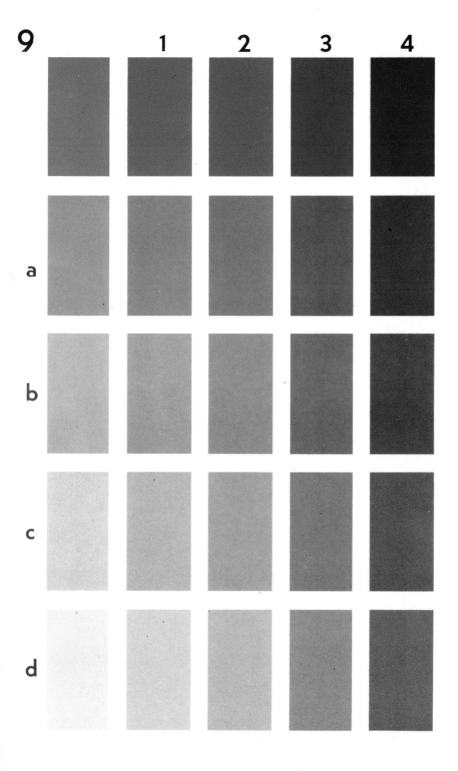

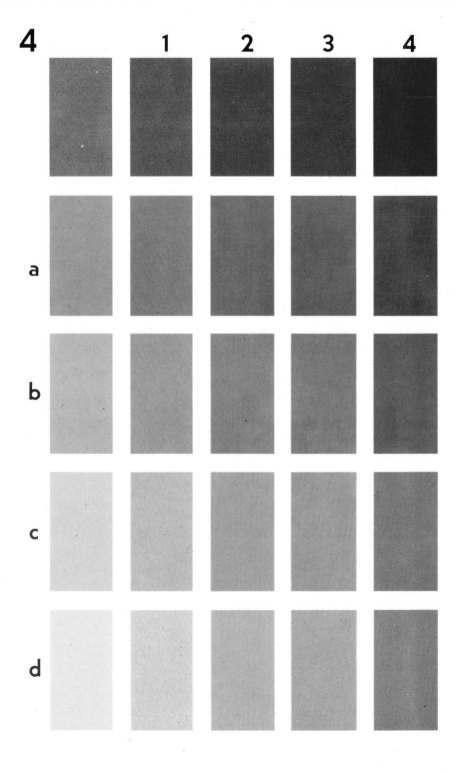

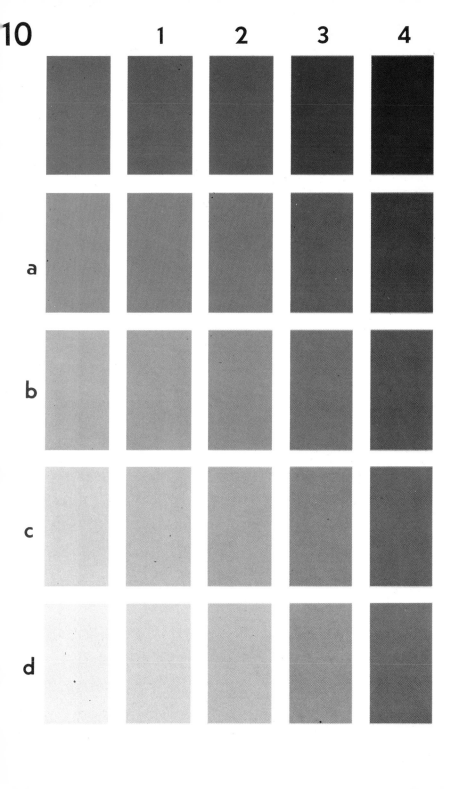

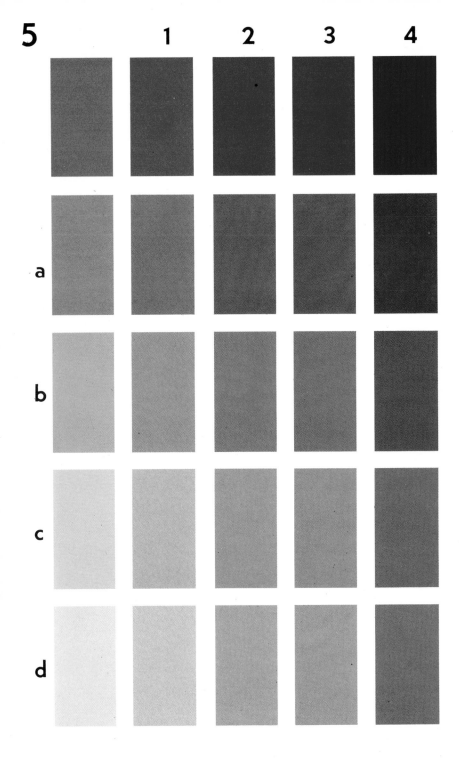

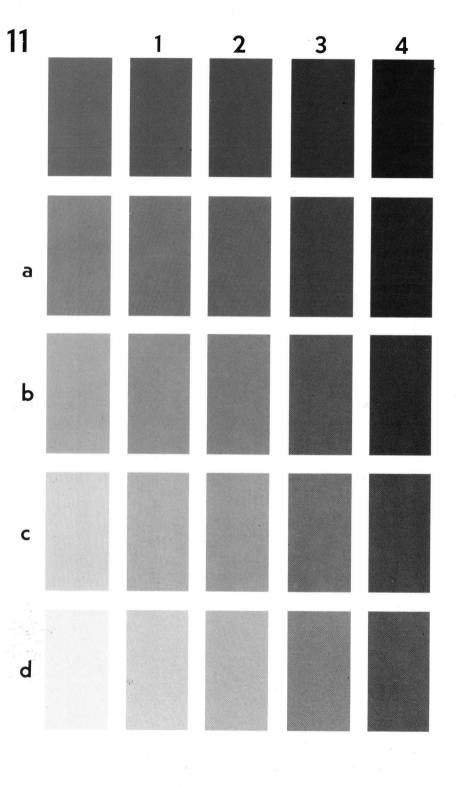

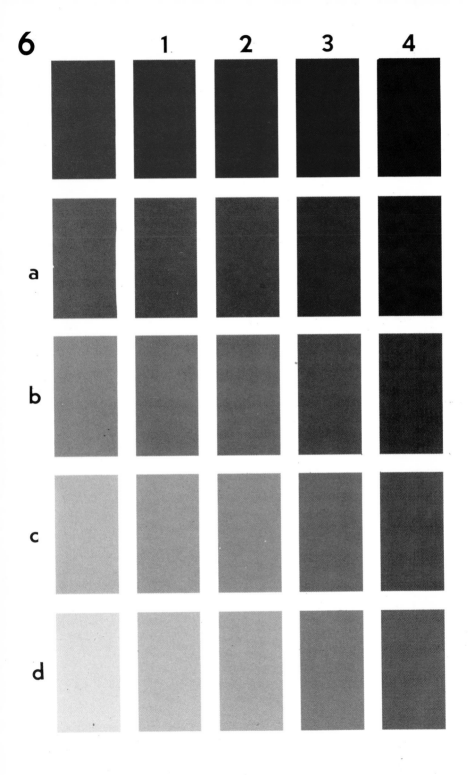

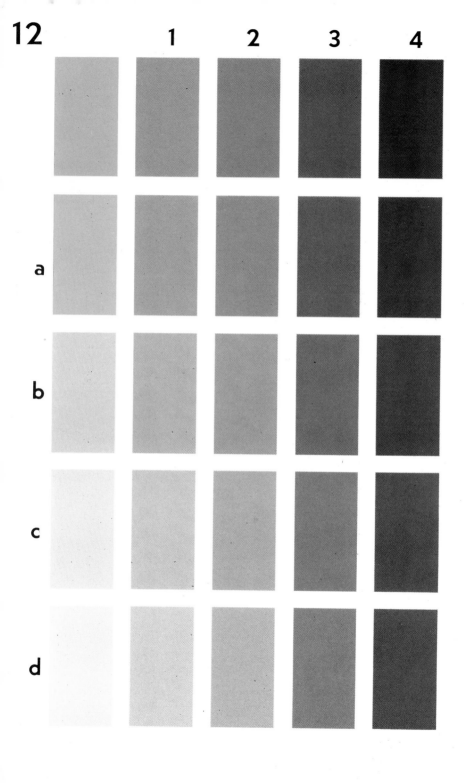

Index

absorption of light, 24–25, 31–32
accents, 29, 34, 37, 54–55
advancing colors, 19, 33
after-image, 25–26
analogous colors, 28, 146
appetite, 11–12, 62–63
association, 11, 19–21, 97, 102, 104–105, 138–139

baby blue, 34, 70–72
baby pink, 21, 34, 70–72
basement, 76
basic hue, 28–30

bathroom, 45, 49
bedroom, 45, 49, 55–61
black, psychology of, 107
blonde, color for, 92
brown hair, color for, 89–90
brunette, color for, 88–89

case histories, 4–6, 12–19, 45–46, 62–63, 76–77, 83–88, 101–106
ceiling, 31, 74, 76, 80
ceramics, 115–121
charts, use of, 143–150
chemical aspects, 135–136
child reaction, 13–16, 18–19, 21–23
color balance, 26–27, 29–31, 34–37
color blindness, 26, 133–134
complementaries, 25–31, 34–37, 47–50, 52–53, 129–130, 136–138,
    145–146
composition, 37–39, 47–50
conditioned reflex, 97–99
contrast, 29–31, 34, 48–49, 68–69, 79
cool colors, 20–21, 26–29, 33–34, 64
cost factor, 51, 54

dilution, 27, 140, 143
dining area, 46, 48–49, 61–66
dishes, 65–66
dominant color, 26–27, 29–30, 34–35, 45
dosage, 23, 27, 29, 138
draperies, 34, 59, 88–90

ego-involvement, 100–103
emotional stability, 6–7, 22
environment, 6–7, 50
exotic, 56, 72
experiments, 9–12, 32

exterior, 49
extrovert, 98

fashionable color, 8, 40–42, 82
fetishes, 104–106
floor covering, 30, 54, 69, 80
fluorescent light, 58
food, 61–62, 66
Fordney and Settle, 32
functional design, 110–112
furniture, 31, 35, 37, 41–44, 48, 54, 57–59, 75–76, 88, 94, 112–115

gray, psychology of, 107–108
guest room, 81–88

habit, 97
harmonious colors, 28–31, 36–38
Hiroshima, 32
home of the future, 121–123
hue, 129, 143–144, 148

illumination, 31, 33, 58–59, 63–64, 66, 73–81
incandescent light, 58
inhibitory reflex, 97–99
introvert, 98

kitchen, 66–70

libido, 98, 100–103
lighting, types of, 37, 58, 64, 74, 79
living room, 48, 51–55

margarine, 62
matching color, 53–54, 147
mixing color, 28, 147–150

neutrals, 24, 30, 35
noncomplementaries, 30
nudes, 61
nursery, 70–71

Pavlov, 97
phobias, 16, 53, 56, 62–63, 104–106
physical aspects, 125–131
physiological aspects, 133–134
Piccard, 32
picture frames, 119
pictures, 115–121
playroom, 76–77
preference tests, 137–140
prestige identification, 100–103
primaries, contradictions of, 5
primaries of light, 128–133
primaries of pigment, 128–133, 147–149
psychological aspects, 135–141

receding colors, 33
redhead, color for, 91
reflection of light, 31–33, 74–76
related colors, 28–29, 53–55, 144
rugs, 54

sculpture, 115, 121
sedatives, 19–23
sensation transference, 45–46, 66

shade, 28–31, 129–130, 144, 149
simultaneous contrast, 134
split color harmonies, 146
stimulants, 19–23
study, 72–76
symbolism, 20, 76, 138

table setting, 65–66
temperature, 31–33
tint, 28–31, 143, 149
tone, 28–31, 130, 144, 150
traumatic experience, 13–19

value, 28

wallpaper, 108–110
walls, 30–31, 37, 48, 52–54, 56–59, 68–69, 76–77, 80, 88–94
warm colors, 19–20, 26–29, 33–34, 49, 64
white hair, color for, 93–94
white, psychology of, 107
work counter, 70
workshop, 78–81